WATERSIDE W

In Wiltshi

Other areas covered in the *Waterside Walks* series include:

Berkshire

Bristol and Bath

Cheshire

Derbyshire

Devon

Essex

Hampshire

Kent

Lancashire

Lincolnshire

Nottinghamshire

Staffordshire

Suffolk

Surrey

Sussex

Warwickshire

Yorkshire

WATERSIDE WALKS
In Wiltshire

Nick Channer

COUNTRYSIDE BOOKS
NEWBURY, BERKSHIRE

Contents

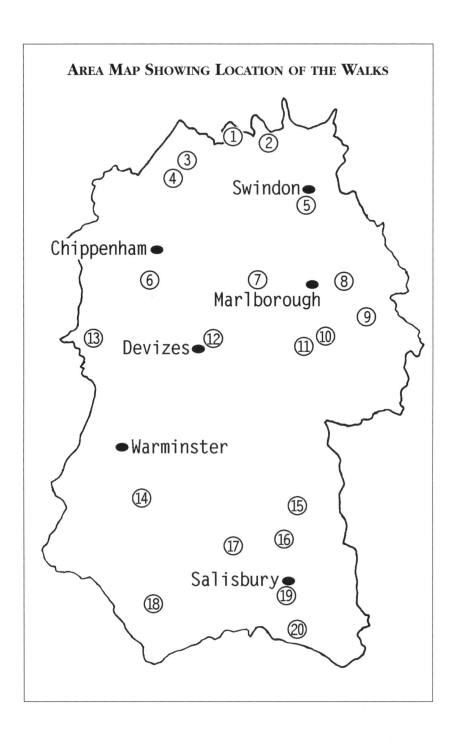

AREA MAP SHOWING LOCATION OF THE WALKS

Walk

Publisher's Note

We hope that you obtain considerable enjoyment from this book; great care has been taken in its preparation. Although at the time of publication all routes followed public rights of way or permitted paths, diversion orders can be made and permissions withdrawn.

We cannot, of course, be held responsible for such diversion orders and any inaccuracies in the text which result from these or any other changes to the routes nor any damage which might result from walkers trespassing on private property. We are anxious though that all details covering the walks are kept up to date and would therefore welcome information from readers which would be relevant to future editions.

INTRODUCTION

The south-east of England may be overrun with housing developments, out-of-town shopping complexes and congested motorways, but a few miles to the west lies a county where you can walk for miles without meeting a soul and savour the stark beauty of a bare, empty landscape seemingly untouched by time.

The county of Wiltshire survives as an unspoilt corner of England where there is strong evidence of early human habitation. Apart from the timeless prehistoric sites, the monoliths and barrows, the great houses and the sweeping chalk downlands, there are belts of richly-coloured woodlands and forest, snug villages and mellow stone cottages. Various rivers and canals thread their way through Wiltshire, and over the years they too have played an important part in shaping the county's varied landscape.

The walks in this book, all of which are circular and include full route-finding instructions, are designed to provide a fascinating insight into the changing character of the county's rural heartland. But hopefully they do much more than just that. The one thing all the routes have in common is that they follow stretches of Wiltshire's loveliest waterways. In the north of the county you can stroll through the vast Cotswold Water Park where lakes and channels stretch for miles in all directions; take a walk along the Thames Path, following the fledgling river close to where it rises; or follow the banks of the disused Thames and Severn Canal which has not been in use for over 70 years.

Running east to west across Wiltshire is the Kennet and Avon Canal which thankfully survives as a lasting monument to the engineering achievements of the pre-railway era. After many years of restoration work, the canal reopened in 1990 and today you can walk its length, following the towpath through glorious Wiltshire countryside. Learn about the history of the canal as you go and enjoy the tranquil scenery it offers. Further south are the valleys of the Nadder, the Wylye, the Till and the Avon – all of them perfect for walking.

Most of the walks feature a welcoming inn at the start of the walk or midway round the route. This enables you to relax and take stock. There are also brief details about where to park and information on places of interest within easy reach of the walk route to help you plan a full day out if you wish.

You don't have to be a serious rambler to tackle the walks in this guide. However, there are often patches of wet ground to be found – even on a short walk of 2 or 3 miles – and some of the routes cross low-lying ground and lush watermeadows which are prone to flooding. Therefore, appropriate footwear is always an important consideration when out walking. A small rucksack to carry rainwear is also recommended, as is a copy of the relevant Ordnance Survey map, which is useful if you want to extend the route and for identifying the main features. A camera is also worth carrying as waterside walks often reveal plenty of wildlife and other fascinating attractions.

Should you prefer to use public transport to get to the start of the walks, some of them are within easy reach of a railway station. For times of trains throughout Wiltshire, call the 24-hour information line on 0345 484950.

Finally, I hope you enjoy these gentle waterside walks which take you to the heart of one of England's loveliest counties. My grateful thanks to Brian Reynolds for his help and advice during the writing of this book. A true friend and a trusted guide.

Nick Channer

A COTSWOLD WATER PARK WALK

This is a classic waterside walk. Following Wiltshire's boundary with Gloucestershire, it explores an extensive network of lakes and channels which is part of the Cotswold Water Park, a vast amenity area which draws locals and visitors from further afield.

The Cotswold Water Park

Somerford Keynes, where the walk begins, is a picturesque village on the Wiltshire and Gloucestershire border. The name appears in a Saxon charter dating back to AD 685, which mentions a ford crossing the Thames.

The Cotswold Water Park is Britain's largest water park and contains more water than the Norfolk Broads. The area is known unofficially as the Cotswold Lake District. Within its boundaries are 132 lakes which have been created by gravel extraction and cover over 30 square miles. The Cotswold Water Park is recognised nationally for the diversity of its wildlife, but it is also the park's very varied range of facilities that attracts people here. You will find picnic and barbecue sites, plenty of parking and access to a network of bridleways, cycleways and footpaths. Walking, angling, sailing, windsurfing, canoeing, jet skiing and horse riding are among the more popular pursuits in the park.

The Cotswold Water Park is a wildlife paradise. Keen ornithologists will identify sand martins, kingfishers, wagtails, dippers, singing warblers and numerous other birds by the lakes and over the watermeadows. Dragonflies are seen everywhere during the lazy days of summer. See if you can spot otters and mink and the even rarer water vole.

The Bakers Arms at Somerford Keynes offers a large car park, traditional ales, a children's garden and plenty of inn food. Bar snacks and a full menu are available every day except Sunday lunchtime, when a traditional roast is served. There is also a garden menu during the summer months. Vegetarians are catered for and there is a range of dishes for children. Telephone: 01285 861298

- **HOW TO GET THERE:** Take the A419 between Swindon and Cirencester or the A429 between Malmesbury and Cirencester and follow the signs for Somerford Keynes.
- **PARKING:** Parking is available for patrons at the Bakers Arms in Somerford Keynes, though please tell the landlord if you are intending to leave a vehicle here while doing the walk. An alternative is to park at the Neigh Bridge Country Park and start the walk at point 5.
- **LENGTH OF THE WALK:** 5¼ miles. Map: OS Landranger 163 Cheltenham and Cirencester (GR 018954).

THE WALK

1. From the Bakers Arms turn right and walk through Somerford Keynes, passing a telephone box and a turning to Cricklade on the left. Veer into Mill Lane and follow it to the edge of the village. Cross what is known as the Spine Road, representing the county boundary between Gloucestershire and Wiltshire at this point, and follow the Thames Path and Lower Mill Estate signs.

2. Follow the tarmac drive between trees and bushes. Soon the first of the lakes featured on this walk edges into view on the left. This is Mill Lake. Pass Lower Mill Farm and note the stripling Thames running beside the track. Keep going until you reach a gate with a sign which

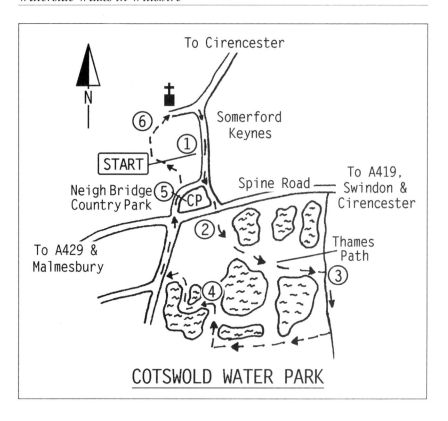

To Cirencester

†

N

⑥

①

Somerford
Keynes

START

Neigh Bridge ⑤
Country Park

CP

Spine Road ——

To A419,
Swindon &
Cirencester

To A429 &
Malmesbury

②

③

Thames
Path

④

COTSWOLD WATER PARK

reads: 'Private land – strictly no public access.' Swing right here and cross the footbridge over the Thames. Follow the path alongside the lake and from here you can see a large barn on the far side. Our walk makes for this landmark later. Continue following the path all the way to two stiles and a sign for Poole Keynes.

3. Turn right here and follow the track alongside the lake and on a breezy day the water can be heard gently lapping the lakeshore. Continue to a stile and maintain the same direction, following the left-hand edge of the field. This stretch of countryside has a timeless feel to it and has not evolved as other cultivated landscapes have. The low-lying ground here is prone to flooding and so therefore has not been ploughed. Make for the far corner of the field and swing right at the waymark. Cross a footbridge and head diagonally across the field, making for the wide gap in the corner. The Swill Brook is seen on the left. Pass a waymark, follow the grassy path and join a stony track at the corner of the lake. Keep going for a few yards, then bear left over a footbridge.

4. This is Howell's Barn, seen earlier in the route. Follow the path, with views of the lake on the left. Cross a stile and follow the lakeside path. This is part of the Swillbrook Lakes Nature Reserve, which lies in the south-west corner of the Cotswold Water Park. Turn right at the lane and cross over at the next main junction.

5. Pass a turning for Neigh Bridge Country Park and turn left just before the village sign for Somerford Keynes (signposted to Ewen). We are now back beside the fledgling Thames, following the lush riverbank. Further on, the paths divide on the bank. Take either path, they soon reunite to run alongside the Thames. Turn right at the footbridge and skirt the field. The church at Somerford Keynes can be seen in the distance. Make for a kissing gate in the field corner; continue in the next field, passing a stile and footbridge. Follow the field edge and a converted barn looms into view now.

6. Leave the Thames Path at the next junction by turning right to cross the field. Look for a stile in the boundary, cross into the next field and pass a huge copper beech tree. Make for a kissing gate and have a look at All Saints' church, located in the north-west corner of Somerford Keynes. This site celebrated 1300 years of Christianity in 1985. Follow the path between walls and hedges and turn right at the road. Bear right at the junction and walk along the village street, back to the Bakers Arms.

PLACE OF INTEREST NEARBY
Keynes Country Park, just east of Somerford Keynes, is open all year and includes a children's beach and play areas. There are lakeside walks, boats for hire, picnic and barbecue sites and day tickets for angling. Contact the Water Park Office on 01285 861459.

CRICKLADE: THE THAMES AND A SECRET CANAL

In an age when alternative means of transportation and the use of public transport are becoming a priority, this fascinating and unusual walk follows communication lines which have long since ceased to be used. From Cricklade the route joins the trackbed of a long abandoned railway into neighbouring Gloucestershire, heading south on a stretch of the disused Thames and Severn Canal to reach the infant Thames, which is very different in character to the river in its lower reaches and through London.

The infant Thames at Cricklade

One of Wiltshire's many small towns, Cricklade was granted a charter in 1155, making it an ancient borough. During the Middle Ages, a Court Leet, a form of local government, was established and is still in existence today. Situated close to the source of the Thames, Cricklade is only a stone's throw from the Roman Ermine Street, upon which the town was once an important military post. Cricklade was described as being 'in lovely surroundings, abounding in all kinds of riches'. The town has fortified Saxon walls, built to protect it from the Danes, and two interesting churches – both totally different in character. St Sampson's is the more well known of the two and is characterised by a tall pinnacled tower which rises above Cricklade and the wide alluvial floor of the Thames valley.

To the north-west, the walk passes a round tower with a slate roof. This was originally the home of the lengthman whose job was to look after the Thames and Severn Canal, ensuring that the level of water did not drop below the required standard. The first boat went through here in 1789; the canal closed to all traffic in 1927 and it was finally abandoned in 1933. In its present derelict state it's difficult to imagine it, but we are told that Captain Horatio Hornblower, the British captain of the Napoleonic wars, the central figure of the novel by C.S. Forester, travelled along this canal en route to London. It may be a muddy, weed-clogged ditch at present, but the Cotswold Canals Trust is masterminding the restoration of both the Thames and Severn Canal and its neighbour, the Stroudwater Navigation, which together make up a 36-mile link between the rivers Severn and Thames.

Midway round the walk is the Crown Inn at Cerney Wick. This family-owned 17th century inn offers a choice of real ales, traditional food and a large garden and patio. Families are welcome and parties of up to 50 people are catered for. Meals and snacks are served every day and there is en suite accommodation. Telephone: 01793 750369.

- **HOW TO GET THERE:** Follow the A419 Cirencester-Swindon road and branch off at the sign for Cricklade.
- **PARKING:** Park at the leisure centre in Cricklade. Approaching from the B4040 turn left by the Vale Hotel to the roundabout and follow the signs.
- **LENGTH OF THE WALK:** 5 miles. Map: OS Landranger 163 Cheltenham and Cirencester (GR 094936).

THE WALK

1. Go to the far end of the car park where there is a galvanised gate. Keep the leisure centre building on the left and follow the bridleway beside the playing fields. Our route is along a disused railway line, part of the Midland and South West Railway which closed to passengers in 1961 and freight traffic in 1964. The old trackbed can be seen running

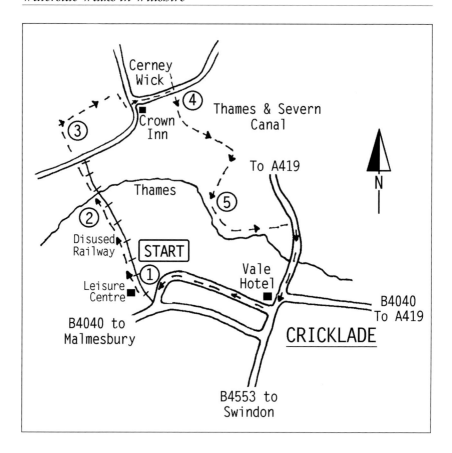

ahead in a straight line between trees and vegetation. In the days when this was a working railway, the next station up the track would have been South Cerney in Gloucestershire. Further on the line is elevated, offering pleasant pastoral views over gentle Wiltshire countryside, and in places you can spot the remains of old culverts. This stretch of the walk is a pleasing reminder of the railway era – gone but not forgotten.

2. Go through the gate and pass over the stripling Thames; soon we reach another gate before continuing between trees and banks of undergrowth. Avoid a turning to Ashton Keynes up ahead; this is where the Thames Path leaves the old railway track. Keep ahead along the trackbed, heading in the direction of South Cerney. Ahead now are the arches of a road bridge, the road leading into Cerney Wick. Continue until you reach a turning for Cerney Wick Lakes on the right.

3. Negotiate the stile and cross the field, looking to the left for a glimpse of the Cotswold Water Park. Cross a footbridge and emerge from the trees at the edge of the lakes. The landscape here is an interesting blend of lakes interspersed with trees and patches of green. Follow the lakeshore, keeping the water on your left, then veer over to the right towards a notice which reads: 'Cotswold Sailing - Private Property. Walkers are requested to keep to the footpaths and exit at waymarked points.' By this notice are two stiles which you should cross. Follow the field edge beside the remains of old pound signs – these were originally used for enclosing animals and may date back to Tudor times. Cross the lane and follow the sign for Cerney Wick. Cross over at the next road and keep the Crown Inn on your right. Cross the River Churn and on the left you can see the distinctive round tower used by the lengthman.

4. Turn right, signposted for Cricklade, and begin the return leg of the walk alongside the old Thames and Severn Canal. On the right along here are the remains of the old stone boundary wall which was built at the same time the canal was dug. Follow the old towpath until eventually you reach the junction with the 19th century North Wilts Canal. Though unrecognisable now, this area of ground was once a basin between two canal systems, equivalent to a railway shunting yard, where boats would gather and cargoes would be dispersed and distributed. There was also an aqueduct over the nearby River Churn.

With traffic on the main road over to your left, head for a galvanised gate and turn right. Keep right, cross a brook and veer left at the fork. Cross a cattle grid and follow the drive towards a private house, once the canal offices. Swing left at the gate and follow the sometimes overgrown path. This stretch can also get waterlogged, so, where flooded, use the logs to pick your way along the path. Our route is now along a branch of the North Wilts Canal, which, in its day, eventually linked up with the Wilts and Berks Canal at Swindon. Cross a high footbridge over a feeder stream and on the left is the vast green expanse of North Meadow, surprisingly open and spacious. The protected 100-acre meadow is a National Nature Reserve and contains many rare plants and flowers, as well as the rare snakeshead fritillary.

5. The Thames Path runs in sharp right at the next footbridge. There was once a canal bridge here and if you look ahead you can picture the original route of the old waterway into Cricklade. Do not cross the bridge; instead, bear left and follow the path between North Meadow and the Thames. Cross the next stile and continue by the river. The church tower at Cricklade is visible now. Follow the path to a wooden gate, with a sign for the Thames Path pointing right. Avoid the path and veer left, crossing the field to a line of trees. Make for the footbridge, swing right in the meadow and keep parallel with the stream. Cross a footbridge and turn right at the road bridge, making for the centre of Cricklade. Walk up the High Street and turn right by the Vale Hotel into Bath Road. Follow the road all the way to the junction. Turn right, then left for the leisure centre car park.

PLACE OF INTEREST NEARBY

Not far away to the north-west, and accessible from Kemble station and the village of Ewen, is the *source of the River Thames*. On reaching it, you will find it is no more than a stream in a Gloucestershire meadow but the walk there is very pleasant and well worth the effort, given that it marks the start of Britain's greatest river.

WALK 3
BRAYDON: AN ANCIENT FOREST AND A PEACEFUL POND

୬ଈୡ

*Explore the varied delights of Ravensroost Wood in the heart of the
Wiltshire countryside before making for the tranquil waters of Braydon
Pond, one of the county's lesser-known aquatic attractions.*

Braydon Pond

Moments after starting this glorious walk you are deep within a silent
forest, picking your way between the trees of the delightfully-named
Ravensroost Wood. Owned and managed by Wiltshire Wildlife Trust
since 1987, this unspoilt woodland lies at the heart of the ancient royal
forest of Braydon which covered an area of 50 square miles and was
one of many similar forests established after the Norman Conquest.
Occasionally used for hunting by the king and his nobles, Braydon was
mainly a source of revenue for the Crown through fines imposed for
violating forest law. The forest eventually lost its royal status during the
reign of Charles I.

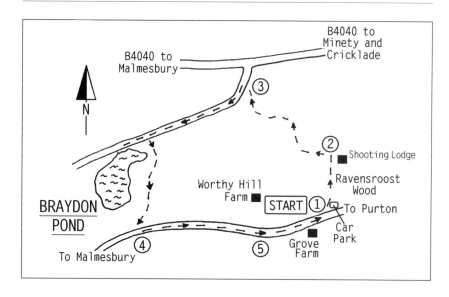

During the 18th century much of the southern part of the wood was felled and cleared for farming, though by 1875 the area had returned to woodland once again. There is a significant difference in the types of plants that grow in the two halves of the wood; the ancient wood has a greater variety of plants than the cleared area.

The shooting lodge in Ravensroost Wood, on the route of the walk, has a wonderful atmosphere. Built in the 1930s to shelter shooting parties, it was later used for holding wood sales and as a woodman's tool store. According to local sources, when shooting parties gathered here and auctions were conducted inside, the participants stayed drinking until the early hours. They then had to be taken home by their horses which knew the way without being told. Today, the hut offers shelter to visitors to the nature reserve.

Braydon Pond represents the largest body of fresh water in North Wiltshire. Though known as a pond, it would be accurate to describe it as a lake. However, the word 'pond' is an ancient one and thus it has remained. Braydon Pond is known for its feathered population and has a large colony of grebe, heron, mallard, mute swan and tufted duck. The pond, once part of a huge private estate, was sold off years ago to pay for death duties. Aircraft used to fly over the water for bombing practice during the Second World War. Walk down to the water's edge and admire the tranquil scene here before continuing the walk.

There are no pubs directly on the route but near to the walk is the

Foresters Arms at Minety. The inn is a freehouse and restaurant with a full à la carte menu, bar snacks and real ales available. Sunday lunch is also served. Telephone: 01793 750901.

- **HOW TO GET THERE:** Ravensroost Wood lies west of the B4696 and south of Minety. From Wootton Bassett and the south follow the B4696 north towards Ashton Keynes. Turn left at the first crossroads, signposted for Minety, and go straight on when the road bends right. Go straight over at the next crossroads towards Charlton and the entrance to the car park is on the right.
- **PARKING:** There is a small free car park at the entrance to Ravensroost Wood.
- **LENGTH OF THE WALK:** 5 miles. Map: OS Landranger 173 Swindon and Devizes (GR 025877).

THE WALK

1. Look at the map in the car park and devise your own route for exploring Ravensroost Wood before beginning the walk proper. Go through the kissing gate to the left of the map and the sign and follow the main track through the forest. Pass a pond on the left and follow the cinder track as it rises through the trees. Suddenly and unexpectedly on the right appears the shooting lodge.

The shooting lodge in Ravensroost Wood

2. Take the path opposite the lodge and walk along to a junction with a wide path. Turn right and shortly you reach an intersection with a bridleway. Bear left here and after a few paces you reach the woodland edge. Skirt the field by keeping to the right-hand boundary, alongside a hedgerow and line of trees. Eventually the path makes for Nineteen Acre Wood. As you head for the cover of the trees, turn sharp right and follow the path just inside the wood, keeping the fields within sight on the right. Follow the clear path through the trees and in due course you reach a field with a water tower seen in the distance. Cross the field to a gate and waymark. Keep the hedge on the right and the water tower over to the left. Pass a corrugated barn by the field corner and go through a gate.

3. Turn left, follow the road and walk down to the edge of Braydon Pond. Then retrace your steps along the lane until you reach a stile at the Pond Lodge estate sign. Follow the tarmac drive ahead through the trees and pass Pond Lodge on the right. Continue as the drive becomes unsurfaced and follow it as it threads its way through the trees. Pass a timber bungalow on the left and avoid turnings either side of the drive. Keep ahead through the woods and eventually you reach a gate and stile.

4. Turn left here and follow the minor road.

5. Pass a track to Worthy Hill Farm and continue on the lane. This road was originally a coaching route between Purton and Malmesbury and although it is said that the verges were cut back in order to deter highwaymen, a more likely explanation for the road width is carts and pedestrians moving from side to side in order to avoid deep ruts. Walk along to Grove Farm on the right and ahead now is Ravensroost Wood. Pass a cottage on the left, go down the hill and turn left into the car park.

PLACE OF INTEREST NEARBY

Lydiard Park, one of Wiltshire's smaller stately homes, near junction 16 of the M4 at Swindon, lies in beautiful parkland and was rescued from ruin by Swindon Corporation in 1943. Attractions include a curious little blue dressing room, elegant ground floor apartments and a 17th century painted window by Abraham Van Linge, which contains over one hundred pieces of glass. The park is wonderful for exploring and in spring the woodlands are carpeted with snowdrops. Telephone: 01793 770401.

WALK 4

MALMESBURY: THE TETBURY AND SHERSTON AVON

Crossing pretty pastures and peaceful watermeadows by the Tetbury and Sherston branches of the River Avon, this very varied ramble never strays far from the charming town of Malmesbury which it keeps within its sights most of the time. The walk finishes by visiting magnificent Malmesbury Abbey, one of Wiltshire's most historic buildings.

The River Avon at Tetbury

Perched high on a rocky promontory and dominated by a splendid late Norman abbey, Malmesbury is one of Wiltshire's most fascinating towns. But there is much more to the place than its impressive setting and great sense of history. A tour of Malmesbury reveals an Anglo-Saxon street plan and a town wall. More than anything, Malmesbury is a perfect example of a Saxon fortified hilltop town dating from about AD 600. Later, in AD 880, Alfred granted the town a charter and constructed defences after recapturing Malmesbury from the Vikings.

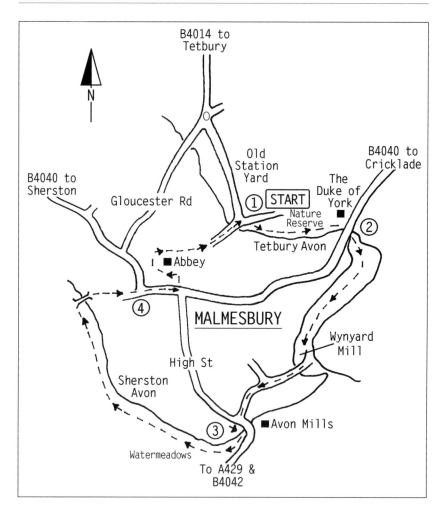

Local tradition suggests that the Abbey and town were founded by a Celtic monk who established a school here. However, historical records indicate that the first Abbot of Malmesbury was Aldhelm in the 7th century. The Abbey, which subsequently became the parish church, was founded as a Benedictine monastery and was once a major European centre of scholarship and learning. Originally there was a square tower surmounted by a spire which was supposedly higher than that of Salisbury Cathedral. The tower collapsed during a storm in about 1500. At the Dissolution of the Monasteries, Malmesbury Abbey was sold to a clothier for little more than £1,500.

Inside the Abbey is the tomb of King Althelstan who was acknowledged as the first King of All England. Choosing Malmesbury as his capital, it was he who commissioned a translation of the Bible into English and donated gifts to the town. The nave is of particular interest, with its ornate roof bosses and 'watching loft'. Outside is the grave of Hannah Twynnoy who died in 1703 aged 33, killed by a tiger which was part of a menagerie visiting the town.

Following the Dissolution, Malmesbury's fortunes began to improve significantly, and, thanks to the endless supply of water around it, the town became an important centre for the manufacture of woollen cloth, lace and silk. Most of the 18th century buildings you see today reflect that chapter in the town's economy.

There are a number of pubs in Malmesbury but one of its quaintest and most popular is the Smoking Dog in the High Street, an 18th century hostelry with stone floors and log fires. Plenty of good food is available every day, and there is a relaxing atmosphere inside. Telephone: 01666 825823.

- **HOW TO GET THERE:** Malmesbury is on the A429, north of junction 17 of the M4.
- **PARKING:** The walk starts at Malmesbury's Old Station Yard car park, where there is plenty of parking. This is located on the north side of the town, off the B4014 Tetbury to Gloucester road.
- **LENGTH OF THE WALK:** 2 miles. Map: OS Landranger 173 Swindon and Devizes (GR 933874).

The Walk

1. Keep the Tetbury branch of the Avon on your right as you leave the car park, with Malmesbury Abbey up on the skyline. Make for the map and information board and swing left here. After a few paces you reach a kissing gate on the right. This is the entrance to the Conygre Mead nature reserve – once the monastery's rabbit warren. Follow the path, with the Abbey gardens visible through the trees on the right. Pass a seat and the Avon is now on your immediate right. Head for the Duke of York pub, cross the road at the next bridge and after a few paces you reach a stile.

2. Cross the watermeadow; the river divides here. Follow the path with the water on your immediate right. Pass the remains of an old railway line, closed in 1962, and keep the Avon on your left. Cross a stile and footbridge and look for a bowling green on the right. Pass Wynyard Mill and on reaching a road called Baskerville, turn right and cross the river bridge. Follow St John Street and cross over at the junction, by the stone pillars in memory of the Malmesbury men who made the supreme sacrifice in the Second World War.

3. Go through the gates and veer left, crossing the Sherston branch of the Avon to the road by Avon Mills. Turn right and then first right through the wooden gate to a stile. Follow the permitted path ahead across the watermeadow, keeping parallel to the river. Walk beneath some willows to a kissing gate and continue ahead across several footbridges. Make for another kissing gate and cross two more footbridges before bearing right in the field corner. Keep left at the fork and follow the path towards the buildings of Malmesbury on the hill. Follow the path down to a stone bridge and continue on the paved path towards the town. Turn right by some lock-up garages, following the path as it climbs towards Malmesbury. Just beyond the sign for Burnivale bear left and climb the steps.

4. Keep right at the top and head towards the Market Cross. Turn left here to visit Malmesbury Abbey. From the front of it, bear right to the Old Bell and then immediately right, following the Cloister Garden sign. The paved path runs round the back of the Abbey, through the garden. Walk along to Abbey House Gardens which are open daily. Teas are also available. Bear left by the entrance, down the path to some steps. At the bottom, keep right, pass the town map and return to the car park.

PLACE OF INTEREST NEARBY

The Cotswolds lie a short distance to the north of Malmesbury. This enchanting corner of England is perfect for walking, with glorious old beechwoods, breezy limestone uplands and views in all directions. Moreton-in-Marsh, Broadway, Burford and Chipping Campden are among the many picturesque towns in the region.

SWINDON: COATE WATER

A diverse country walk combining the natural and man-made attractions of a popular country park close to Swindon with the green fields of rural Wiltshire.

Coate Water

If you don't know Swindon that well, you might be surprised to learn that on the town's doorstep lies a most attractive country park which is ideal for relaxing and exploring on foot. The Coate Water Country Park is located immediately to the south of Swindon, between the town and the M4 motorway. Its setting may not sound all that inviting, but once you're there, it's so quiet and peaceful that you feel you're in the heart of the countryside.

At the centre of the park lies a 56-acre reservoir, built in the 1820s as a head-water tank for the old Wiltshire and Berkshire Canal. Much later, during the 1970s, a smaller lake was created as a flood storage lagoon and in 1976 this became Wiltshire's first local nature reserve. Virtually the whole site has been declared a Site of Special Scientific

Interest, affording the wildlife and wildflower meadows complete protection. Deer and foxes are often spotted in the area and a large heronry has been established in the dead trees. In the wetter areas of woodland, look for willow and ash, with oak and birch seen on the drier ground. The reedbeds are a valuable habitat for spring and summer waterfowl, as well as supporting a varied assortment of dragonflies.

Near its starting point, the walk passes close to Coate Farm where the well-known 19th century writer and journalist Richard Jefferies was born. It was Jefferies who famously wrote: 'They only know a country who are acquainted with its footpaths. By the roads, indeed, the outside may be seen; but the footpaths go through the heart of the land.' Very much a loner, Jefferies spent much of his time walking on the Wiltshire Downs and in the Surrey and Sussex countryside. In his book *Wiltshire Villages*, Brian J. Woodruffe mentions one of the county's most famous sons, as well as Coate Water 'which figures as a weedy mere in Jefferies' writings'.

The Calley Arms at Hodson, just over halfway round the walk, offers a selection of home-made food, a range of real ales, up to 15 English country wines and 60 malt whiskies. There is also a traditional Sunday roast and various snacks. Outside is a popular beer garden. Telephone: 01793 740350.

- **HOW TO GET THERE:** Turn south off the A4259, following the signs for the Coate Water Country Park. Approaching from junction 15 of the M4, follow the A419 north to the next roundabout before turning left on the A4259.
- **PARKING:** There is a pay and display car park within the boundaries of the country park.
- **LENGTH OF THE WALK:** 5 miles. Map: OS Landranger 173 Swindon and Devizes (GR 176826).

THE WALK

1. Before leaving the car park have a look at the building housing the Ranger Centre and study the carved faces over the lintels – the hallmark of a noted local bricklayer around the turn of the century, who used this particular design in much of his work. Keep the building on your left and follow the path through the trees, signposted to Barbury Castle, Hodson and Chiseldon. Look over to the right for a good view of the listed diving tower, a classic 1930s feature. Keep the model railway on

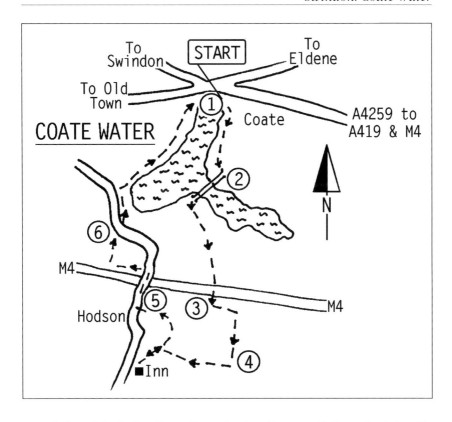

your left and look for Coate Farm in the distance. Follow the lakeside path until you reach a main bridge.

2. Veer left here, away from the water's edge, and follow the path into a copse. Pass a map showing the route of a popular walk between Coate and Hodson. Further on, look for a sign on the right – 'Cicely's Bridge – Built 1820. "The low parapet of the bridge affords a seat – one of Cicely's favourite haunts..." from Richard Jefferies' novel *Round About a Great Estate* (1880).' The picture depicts Cicely sitting on the bridge. Keep going, following the right-hand edge of a field to a stile close to the motorway. Cut across the corner of the field to the next stile and take the footbridge over the M4.

3. Go through a galvanised gate and follow the woodland path signposted to Hodson. This part of the walk follows the disused trackbed of the old Midland and South West Railway, which opened in

On the way to Hodson

the 1870s, closed in 1961 and ran from Cheltenham to Andover. It was used by servicemen of the 101st Airborne Division who were based locally prior to D-Day in 1944. Cut diagonally across the field to a stile and then head up the slope through the trees.

Skirt the next field, keeping to its right-hand boundary. Look for a sign for Hodson in the corner, and take the path down the slope and round to the right, descending into the valley. Make for a stile and follow the path down between trees and bushes, cutting through the enclosed valley. Rolling green flanks and grassy outcrops characterise the scene here. Pass over a brook and bear immediately right.

4. Follow the path alongside the water and make for a sign for Barbury Castle, Hodson and the Calley Arms. Veer left here and follow the path up the field, between the bushes. Cross a stile and continue up the slope to the pub. From the Calley Arms retrace your steps down the path, veer over to the left a little and aim for a stile set against the woodland. Cross it and follow the path as it climbs quite steeply through the trees. Bear left at the field edge and follow the perimeter for some time. Pass a stile and curve right in the field corner. Look for a stile and exit to the road.

5. Turn right and pass the entrance to Burderop Park on the left. This was the family seat of the Calley family. Go down the lane, pass the route of the old railway and cross over the motorway again. Once across it, bear sharp left to join a narrow path. Make for a stile and continue with the M4 on your left. Head for the trees and turn right, keeping the woodland on your left. Pass several sarsen stones in the field corner and emerge at the road on a bend.

6. Go straight ahead through the trees and after a few paces you join a parallel path on the right. Look out for an impressive view of Coate Water along here. Follow the path alongside the road and before long you reach a stile and a map of the area. Keep right here and follow the main path through the park. In due course, the diving platform is seen ahead. Pass the platform and follow the path back to the car park.

PLACE OF INTEREST NEARBY
Coate Water has boats for hire and a coarse fishery day ticket is available. The Ranger Service offers a selection of talks and activities for clubs, societies, community groups and colleges. There is also a programme of walks and events open to everyone throughout the year. There are special activities, too, for children during the school holidays to enable them to learn more about the countryside. Facilities at Coate Water include a café, play area, pitch and putt, orienteering, bird hides, model railway and barbecue hire. For more information call the Ranger Centre on 01793 490150.

BY THE AVON AT LACOCK

This is a short but fascinating walk around the beautifully preserved village of Lacock. It begins by crossing a green and fertile landscape, passing alongside the placid waters of the meandering Avon. Soon you reach Lacock, a jewel among Wiltshire villages, where the charming scene is dominated by old timber buildings, gabled roofs and a maze of quaint streets. End the walk by visiting the splendid Abbey.

The Avon

Cared for by the National Trust, Lacock is one of Wiltshire's most beautiful villages – a perfect example of medieval England. Its ancient streets are packed with tourists in summer and so neat and well-preserved is the place that you almost feel as if you are visiting a museum. However, thriving Lacock most certainly is real but perhaps the best time to explore it is autumn or winter when the crowds are fewer and the place seems more like a genuine village. The buildings date mainly from the 13th and 14th centuries and the church is 15th century.

If you've never been to Lacock before, you might recognise it as the backdrop to several films and television series, and the village featured prominently in the BBC's adaptation of Jane Austen's *Pride and Prejudice* in 1996 when it became the fictional home of Elizabeth Bennet and her family. Very few changes were required for the filming, though the main street was covered with turf and gravel for a week and the postbox was disguised as the village pump. Its shell had to be removed twice a day at collection time! When filming was completed the BBC gave the turf to local residents. Lacock has also featured in *Moll Flanders, Emma* and *Randall and Hopkirk (Deceased)*.

After exploring the village, pay a visit to Lacock Abbey, which lies directly on the route of the walk. Founded in 1232 for Augustinian nuns, the Abbey was converted to a house in the 16th century. Later it passed by marriage to the Talbot family. William Henry Fox Talbot, who was one of the early pioneers of photography, is buried in the cemetery in West Street. The National Trust owns both the Abbey and the Fox Talbot Museum of Photography.

There are several pubs in Lacock. The George Inn in West Street is one of the oldest buildings in the village and dates from 1361. The face of George II is depicted on the pub sign. Bar and restaurant food is served all week. Beers include Wadworth 6X and outside is a garden with seating and a patio. The George also does accommodation. Telephone: 01249 730263. The Red Lion in Lacock's High Street dates from the 1700s and includes exposed timbers and a large open fireplace. Home-made dishes are available throughout the week, food is served outdoors during the summer and children are welcome. The Red Lion also has four en suite bedrooms. Telephone: 01249 730456.

- **HOW TO GET THERE:** Lacock is just off the A350 Melksham to Chippenham road. Approaching from either direction, it is clearly signposted.
- **PARKING:** The walk starts from the large car park just south of the village.
- **LENGTH OF THE WALK:** 2 miles. Map: OS Landranger 173 Swindon and Devizes (GR 916684).

THE WALK

1. From the car park turn right and follow the road round to the right. Lacock Abbey edges into view on the left. Follow the raised bridge towards the stone road bridge, cross it and look for a stone stile on the left.

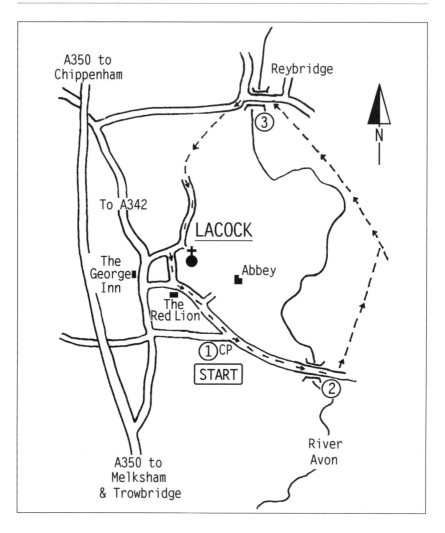

2. Begin crossing the field, with the Abbey glimpsed through the trees on the left now. A third of the way across the pasture, veer over to the right to a footbridge and stile. Turn left and skirt the field, continuing ahead in the next pasture. Power lines can be seen to the right, and in the distance the partly tree-clad slopes of Bowden Hill; to the left are pretty parkland views. Cross to a stile, with the Avon looping round in front of you. Go forward with the river on your left. Cross a stile under some willow trees and continue along the riverbank. Keep ahead to the next stone road bridge, by some thatched cottages.

Lacock

3. Turn left, then left again at the junction. As the road bends right, go straight on up a tarmac path to a kissing gate. Cross the field to a lane, turn left and walk down to a ford. Follow the road into the centre of Lacock and on reaching the church, turn right. Pass the Carpenter's Arms and note the sign referring to mail coaches. Turn left immediately beyond the inn into East Street and walk along to the Red Lion. Bear left opposite the inn and follow the road out of the village, passing the entrance to Lacock Abbey and the museum. Keep to the path on the right of the road and follow it through light woodland, back to the car park.

PLACES OF INTEREST NEARBY
Bowood House and Gardens near Calne are well worth a visit. The house is set in idyllic parkland with terraced gardens and a lake and includes collections of heirlooms, porcelain and paintings. There is also a gift shop, garden centre, licensed restaurant and tearoom. Telephone: 01249 812102.

Corsham Court at Corsham is the home of the Methuen family and includes English furniture by Robert Adam and Chippendale. The park was designed by 'Capability' Brown and features pleasant gardens and a Gothic cold bath house. Telephone: 01249 701610.

AVEBURY AND THE RIVER KENNET

The picturesque village of Avebury is widely recognised as one of Britain's most important Bronze Age sites and is famous throughout the world for its ancient standing stones. Beginning by the stones in the centre of Avebury, the walk soon leaves the village to cut across a primitive, windswept landscape littered with remote monuments to the past. Midway round, the route coincides with a pretty stretch of the River Kennet near where it rises, before heading back cross-country to Avebury.

Silbury Hill

Charles II was recommended by John Aubrey to visit Avebury in 1663 because '...it does as much exceed in greatness the renowned Stonehenge as a Cathedral doeth a parish church...'

Virtually whatever time of the year you visit Avebury, there are always visitors to be seen here. It is that sort of place. In the summer, coachloads of tourists flock to the site, photographing the village and peering at the stones with curious, puzzled expressions. Given its status as a World Heritage Site, ranking in importance alongside the likes of the Taj Mahal, it's hardly surprising that it draws such large crowds. Consisting of a sizeable outer bank and inner ditch, Avebury is acknowledged by historians as one of Europe's most important Neolithic sites. The brooding standing stones make up one of the largest remaining henge monuments, even older than Stonehenge. It is an extraordinary mystical place and the only way to appreciate it is to go there.

Avebury was at the centre of controversy in the autumn of 2000 when it emerged that the village was partly destroyed by the archaeologist and marmalade heir Alexander Keiller who acquired it in 1934. What we see today is largely his creation as he made considerable changes – demolishing cottages, blowing up trees and removing fences. His main objective was to remove any sign of human habitation from within the stone circle, a policy later adopted by the National Trust, the site's owner. Keiller and his team of workers jacked up fallen sarsen stones and created the circle as we know it.

The walk passes close to another legendary landmark on its return leg. Built 4,600 years ago, Silbury Hill is the largest man-made mound in prehistoric Europe. Constructed on a spur of natural chalk, this vast engineering project involved millions of hours of labour, though its precise purpose is still a mystery.

The Red Lion at Avebury is a traditional thatched pub with benches at the front and offers lunchtime and evening meals. There are usually two guest ales, as well as Wadworth 6X, IPA and Morland Old Speckled Hen. The menu includes traditional snacks such as baguettes, jacket potatoes, salads, soup, filled Yorkshire puddings and quiche. Pies and fish feature among the more substantial dishes. The inn also does bed and breakfast. Telephone: 01672 539266.

- **HOW TO GET THERE:** Avebury lies on the A4361 to the west of Marlborough. Approaching from the south (the A4, A361, A4361 junction) take the road towards Swindon, avoid the main car park on the left and turn left for Avebury village centre.
- **PARKING:** Use the free car park in the centre of Avebury, located in the High Street opposite the Henge shop and village post office.
- **LENGTH OF THE WALK:** 3¼ miles. Map: OS Landranger 173 Swindon and Devizes (GR 101698).

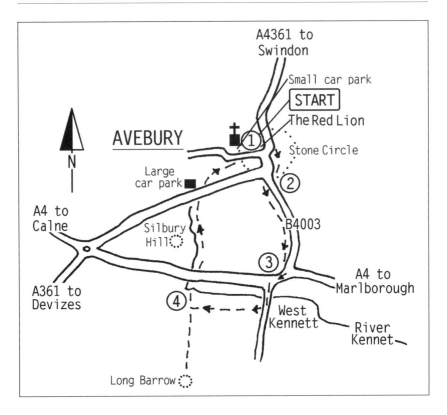

THE WALK

1. Turn left out of the car park, head along to the main road by the Red Lion and cross over to the little gate. Walk ahead between the stones, following the path through the beech trees to another small gate.

2. Exit to the road, cross over, go through the gate and follow the Stone Avenue which cuts between the stones. Make for the bottom of this elongated field and look for a gate on the left. Follow the field edge, with the B4003 on the left, and head for a stile. Cross over to the road and follow it in a southerly direction. On reaching the A4, turn right and take the first left turn into the small village of West Kennett (note the spelling differs slightly from that of the river).

3. Cross the River Kennet and then swing right to join a track. Now the unmistakable outline of Silbury Hill edges into view. Head for a stile and gate and keep ahead, with the fence and field boundary on your right. On reaching a clear path on a bend, you have a choice. To visit the West Kennett Long Barrow bear left; to continue the walk, go straight on. Follow the well-used path round to the right, recross the Kennet and turn left at the A4.

4. Cross over to a gate and path signposted Avebury. Keep the river and Silbury Hill on your left, go through a gate and continue ahead. Cross several stiles, pass a river crossing and follow the path all the way to the A4361. Cross over to Avebury car park, join the path and walk along to the village centre. Turn right and return to the High Street car park.

PLACES OF INTEREST NEARBY

Avebury Manor is in the care of the National Trust and well worth a look. The present building dates from the early 16th century and includes some striking Queen Anne alterations and Edwardian renovation. The topiary and flower gardens contain medieval walls, ancient box and numerous compartments. The house and gardens are open between April and October. Telephone: 01672 539388.

The Alexander Keiller Museum in Avebury contains one of the most important prehistoric archaeological collections in Britain. Open daily. Telephone: 01672 539250.

Avebury Stone Circle

WALK 8

AXFORD: ALONG THE KENNET
❧

From the placid waters of the Kennet, this varied woodland and valley walk makes for densely wooded country above the river before heading east towards Ramsbury Manor. The Kennet's varied wildlife is one of the key attractions on this splendid ramble.

The River Kennet at Axford

Close to the border with Berkshire and about 3 miles east of Marlborough lies the charming linear village of Axford, its main street running parallel to the meandering River Kennet. The oldest buildings are to be found to the south of the road and date back to the 17th century. A chapel of ease dedicated to St Michael was built here in 1856 and was served from Ramsbury. Until 1940 there was no right of marriage here and Axford couples were forced to travel elsewhere to tie the knot.

The Kennet is one of Wiltshire's loveliest rivers and a stroll along its banks is a delight at any time of the year. All manner of wildlife can be seen here, including black swans and Canada and Brent geese. This scenic stretch of the river at Axford is also the setting for the first established fishery on the Kennet nearest the source. Anglers fish here in search of native brown trout, grayling and occasional pike.

With the threat of pollution greatly diminished, otters are being encouraged back to the Kennet. This elusive and enigmatic creature has long endeared itself to adults and children alike and the return of the otter to this river system is a feather in the cap of conservationists. The presence of otters in a river reflects a clean and healthy environment. Young kingfishers may be seen on this stretch too, but they don't nest here, unlike the same pair of swans which have nested on the Kennet here for many years.

The 17th century Red Lion at Axford enjoys lovely views across the valley. Fresh fish and game (in season) feature on the chalkboard, as do many other appetising dishes. Home-made pies and various platters are also available. Food is served every day and there is usually a good range of beers. Telephone: 01672 520271. Alternatively, try the Horseshoe at neighbouring Mildenhall, reopened in 1952 after losing its licence for serving drinks on a Sunday while villagers should have been in church. A good range of food and drinks is available. Telephone: 01672 514725.

- **HOW TO GET THERE:** Axford lies north of the A4 between Marlborough and Hungerford. Approaching from Marlborough turn off at the sign for Stitchcombe and continue to Axford.
- **PARKING:** There is a free car park in Axford's main street, towards the eastern end.
- **LENGTH OF THE WALK:** 5 miles. Map: OS Landranger 174 Newbury and Wantage (GR 241701).

THE WALK

1. Turn left out of the car park and walk along the road. Pass the Red Lion and turn left into Stone Lane. The lane cuts between several thatched cottages and pretty houses. Follow the lane between brick and flint walls, cross over the River Kennet and turn right at the next junction. Follow the lane to a sign for Coombe Way and bear left here over a stile.

2. Walk along to the buildings of Coombe Farm and head up the lane, following it as it climbs up through woodland. Carpets of bluebells add a dash of colour all around in the early summer. Make for a galvanised

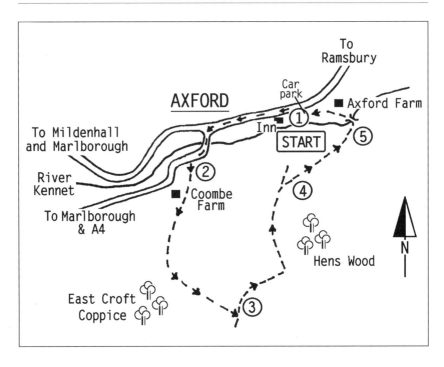

gate and veer right over a double stile here. Turn right, then almost immediately left along the field edge. Make for the corner, cross the stile and continue in a southerly direction along the woodland edge. Keep the field on your left initially. Avoid a stile and a path on the left at the field corner and continue deeper into the woods. Pass a reassuring waymark on one of the trees and keep to the main path until you reach a track on a wide bend. Bear left here and soon merge with a track coming in from the right. Make for a barrier, then turn immediately left before the second barrier. There is also a turning on the right here.

3. Follow the path through the trees, taking the first obvious wide path on the right. There are open fields on the left along here. Keep to the main path, following it within the boundaries of the wood. Soon there is dense woodland on the right. On reaching the field corner, turn left and keep the field on your left. Make for the next field corner and turn right, following the wide track along the woodland edge. Head through a tunnel of trees and descend into the valley. There are pleasant views between the trees.

4. Look for a path on the right, running up by a galvanised gate, and follow it along the lower slopes of the hillside. Pass a path running sharp left across the field and further on your surroundings become more wooded, with thick vegetation lining the route. Drop down to a bend. Along the track a mound is visible, indicating the site of a long abandoned chapel. Turn left on this bend and walk down to the Kennet, crossing the wide, fast-flowing river at a particularly scenic spot.

5. Cross a stile and follow the raised path across the field towards Axford Farm. Keep to the left of the farm, cross the river at the next bridge and keep the water on your left. Initially the path runs beside the river before cutting away to the right to reach a line of trees. Go between them, maintaining the same direction, and head for a stile in the far fence. The river, seen meandering through the fields below, forms a charming picture here. Join the woodland path and follow it to the road. Turn left and return to the car park in Axford.

PLACE OF INTEREST NEARBY
The delightful town of *Marlborough* is only a short drive away and perfect for shopping, exploring on foot or relaxing over a civilised afternoon tea at the renowned Polly Tearooms. As well as visiting the shops and the church, you can discover a fascinating rabbit warren of passages and alleyways behind the handsome shopfronts and half-timbered buildings of Marlborough High Street.

CANALSIDE WALKING AT GREAT BEDWYN

From the village of Great Bedwyn, a noted stop on the Paddington railway line, this superb walk starts off alongside the Kennet and Avon Canal then cuts through the extensive mixed woodland of Bedwyn Brail and Wilton Brail, eventually reaching the canal again near Crofton, for a delightful homeward stretch along the towpath.

The Kennet and Avon Canal at Great Bedwyn

The name Bedwyn is thought to come from the Wiltshire dialect word 'bedwine' or 'bedwind', a term used to describe the wild clematis which is native to the county. The 11th century church of St Mary the Virgin contains an effigy of Jane Seymour's father, John. The Seymour family lived in nearby Savernake Forest. Great Bedwyn is also famous for its local stonemason. Pause for a few moments to look at its assortment of gravestones and memorials on the pavement, some bearing witty and amusing verses.

Completed in 1810, the 87-mile Kennet and Avon Canal took 16 years to construct. The final bill was in the region of one million pounds. With 104 locks and many other awesome engineering features, the canal is regarded as a jewel of 18th and 19th century engineering. It was built to provide a direct trade link between London and Bristol, thus avoiding the treacherous south coast route. The canal eventually became redundant, thanks to the nationalisation of Britain's railway network in the late 1940s. But the Kennet and Avon's dedicated armies of supporters were determined not to let it die.

Restored over many years, the canal was eventually reopened by Her Majesty the Queen at Devizes in 1990 and today the Kennet and Avon is a vibrant waterway once more – the popular haunt of walkers, fishermen and narrowboat enthusiasts. These days, you can walk along its towpath all the way from Reading to Bristol – and there are no hills to spoil your enjoyment!

If time permits, extend this walk slightly in order to see the restored Crofton Pumping Station and Wilton Water, an 8-acre reservoir rising from natural springs and supplying water to the canal's summit level. Designed by Boulton and Watt and reopened by Sir John Betjeman following major restoration work, Crofton pumps water from the reservoir into the canal. Superseded by electricity in 1958, the 19th century steam engines are well worth a visit when the pumping station is open to the public.

The Cross Keys at Great Bedwyn makes an ideal refreshment stop. Fresh home-made food is available every day, from soup and sandwiches to lasagne, not forgetting the popular roast on Sundays. Children's meals are also available. Real ales on offer include London Pride and Wadworth 6X. Telephone: 01672 870678.

- **HOW TO GET THERE:** Situated on the Wiltshire/Berkshire border, Great Bedwyn lies a couple of miles from the A338 Hungerford to Salisbury road. The village also has a railway station.
- **PARKING:** There is room to park in the vicinity of the railway station.
- **LENGTH OF THE WALK:** 5¼ miles. Map: OS Landranger 174 Newbury and Wantage (GR 278645).

THE WALK

1. Leaving the car park, walk up to the junction then cross the railway line and the Kennet and Avon Canal. There is a good view of the church tower on the right. Turn right at the site of the old Great

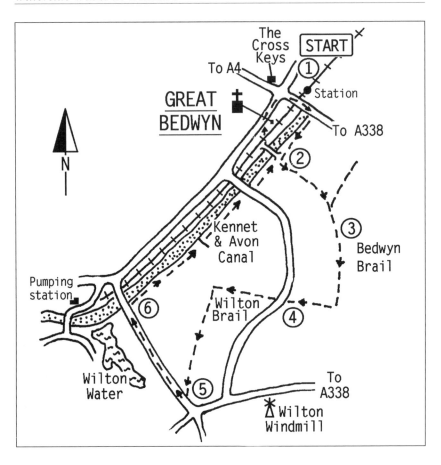

Bedwyn wharf; coal would have been transported here from the Somersetshire Coal Canal. Follow the towpath, more than likely passing an assortment of moored narrowboats along the way. The church of St Mary the Virgin can be seen on the opposite bank.

2. At the next bridge, just before the lock, turn left through a gate and head up the field slope to a line of mature trees and a fence on the right. Make for the field corner and look for a little path running off into a belt of woodland on the left. The path looks rather inviting but sadly is not our route. We must save this delight for another day. Continue ahead skirting the field and keeping the thick hedgerow and trees on the right. Make for the field corner and plunge into the woodland, soon reaching a grassy clearing.

3. Veer over to the right to join a broad grassy path. Pass over a junction of tracks and paths and continue ahead, signposted 'Windmill'. Follow a clear, firm track through the trees. Continue along the track until you reach a sign for Wilton Brail. Turn right and follow the grassy woodland ride which can be seen undulating ahead. Descend to a squeeze stile and go straight on across a tree-fringed field towards the next section of the path.

4. Cross a road and continue ahead between the trees of Wilton Brail. Go up the slope between the trees and descend towards the edge of the field. Veer over to the left and continue through the woodland, passing a few sturdy oaks. Follow the main path, noting the white waymarks. Pick your way between the trees to reach the woodland edge. Over to the right at this point is Tottenham House, ancestral home of the Ailesbury family. Also visible from here is Wilton Windmill. Make for a stile in the boundary hedge and continue on the next section of path. There are good downland views along here. Go down the field, under some power lines and turn sharp right at a track which is an old Roman road.

Great Bedwyn church

5. Go up the track and the buildings of Wilton can be seen down below. Ahead is the outline of Crofton Pumping Station, seen against the rolling downland slopes. Follow the track between trees and high hedges. On reaching the canal you have a choice of routes.

6. To visit Crofton, cross the canal and the railway and then follow the lane to the pumping station. Recross the railway and the canal at this point, have a look at Wilton Water and walk back along the towpath. The main walk now heads back towards Great Bedwyn, passing an isolated single-storey dwelling beside the towpath. Pass several bridges and gradually the buildings of Great Bedwyn edge into view. As you start to draw level with the church, cross the canal at the footbridge, pass over the Kennet and go through two white gates with the railway in between. Follow the path towards the church and make for the main door. On leaving it, turn right, walk along the street and return to the station.

PLACES OF INTEREST NEARBY

Wilton Windmill, to the south of Great Bedwyn, is famous for being the oldest working windmill in Wessex. It was originally constructed in 1821 following the loss of five local windmills when the Kennet and Avon Canal was built. Restored in the 1960s, the windmill is usually open on Sunday and bank holiday afternoons between Easter and September. Telephone: 01672 870427.

Crofton Pumping Station, just off the route of the walk, has an interesting display of steam engines. It is open from Easter to September. Telephone: 01672 870300.

WOOTTON RIVERS: CANAL TOWPATH AND COLUMN RIDE

A very pleasant mix of downland, parkland, forest and canal awaits you on this glorious walk which begins in a classic Wiltshire village. The route is quite lengthy but there is the option to shorten it if desired.

Burbage Wharf

Before starting the walk, take a stroll through the delightful village of Wootton Rivers. Have a look at St Andrew's church by following the long enclosed path leading to its entrance. The church clock is worth closer scrutiny. In fact, there are three faces: two are conventional but the third displays the words 'Glory be to God' around the edge of the dial instead of numerals. The design dates back to 1911 and is the work of the amusingly-named Jack Spratt, an eccentric countryman who established himself locally as an amateur clockmaker. To commemorate the coronation of George V, Wootton Rivers decided to provide the church with a clock, though the idea was greeted with indifference, the sense

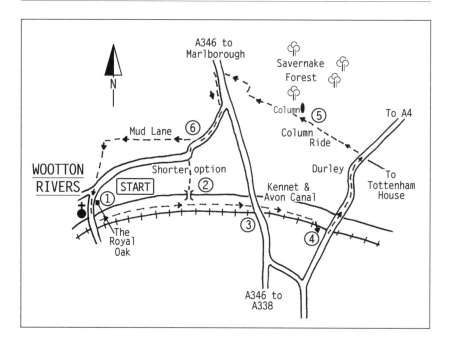

of apathy in the village compounded by a distinct lack of funds. Jack Spratt came to the rescue and offered to make the clock for nothing, using bits of scrap iron, steel, brass and lead.

The lock at Wootton Rivers and this stretch of the Kennet and Avon Canal appeared some years ago in the television series *The River* starring David Essex. The story was set on the Thames, though it was decided to use Wootton Rivers as the river was considered too busy for filming.

Midway round, the walk passes beneath the wooded canopy of Savernake Forest, deliciously cool on a hot summer's day. You might say that one wood looks much like the next and you'd be right. What sets this corner of the forest apart from the rest is the stately Column Ride which extends for almost two miles between the graceful façade of Tottenham House, ancestral home of the Ailesbury family, and an elegant classical monument standing amidst the trees. On reaching the column you will see from reading one of several inscriptions that it was built by Thomas Bruce in memory of his uncle Charles Bruce, a former Earl of Ailesbury who 'left to him these estates and procured for him the barony of Tottenham'. The inscription also refers to George III who conferred upon Thomas Bruce the honour of an earldom.

The Royal Oak at Wootton Rivers serves food seven days a week and among the dishes are steak and Guinness pie, lasagne and steak. Home-made soup, sandwiches and ploughman's are also available. Beers include 6X and Ushers. The inn is thatched and timbered and inside there is a heavily beamed bar. Telephone: 01672 810322.

- **HOW TO GET THERE:** Wootton Rivers lies to the south of Marlborough and can be reached from either the A346 or the A345.
- **PARKING:** There is a free car park off the main street in Wootton Rivers.
- **LENGTH OF THE WALK:** 9 miles (shorter option 3½ miles). Map: OS Landranger 173 Swindon and Devizes (start and end of walk) and Landranger 174 Newbury and Wantage (GR 197628).

THE WALK

Note: Strong footwear is advisable for this walk (both routes) – Mud Lane at point 6 is aptly named.

1. Having walked through the village to the canal, cross the carriage bridge and turn left to join the towpath. Follow it to the next road bridge by a large house with tile-hung elevations and continue to Brimslade Lock, part of the Wootton Rivers flight which was restored in the early 1970s. Several hundred yards beyond the lock you reach the next bridge. For the shorter route cross the bridge, keep right at the junction and join up with the main walk at Mud Lane (point 6).

2. Continue on the towpath beyond Cadley Lock, following it over sometimes muddy ground and through isolated, well-wooded countryside. On this stretch you are climbing to the summit level of the canal which is 450 ft above sea level. After Crofton, several miles to the east, it drops gradually all the way to the Thames at Reading.

3. Follow the towpath to Burbage Wharf, built in the early 19th century by the Earl of Ailesbury. The wooden crane seen across the water is an authentic replica of the original and dates back to 1971. The original crane had to be demolished as it was considered unsafe but drawings were made of it which enabled the Royal Electrical and Mechanical Engineers (REME) to produce an exact copy.

Pass under the bridge at Burbage Wharf and follow the towpath beneath the branches of overhanging trees – a pleasantly shaded section of the walk. Keep going until you approach Bruce Tunnel. The

51

502 ft tunnel is named after the local landowner Thomas Bruce, Earl of Ailesbury, who insisted that the tunnel be built here. John Rennie suggested building a tunnel further south but the cost proved prohibitive. Go up the concrete steps and under the railway bridge, following the path to the road.

4. On the right is the former Savernake Forest Hotel, which was once owned by the British actor Richard Johnson. The building is now home to the Savernake Corporate Development Centre. Follow the road over the railway; hard to believe it now but there used to be two railway stations here – Savernake High Level and Savernake Low Level. Near this point two lines crossed – the GWR line and the Midland and South West Railway line.

The Column Ride through Savernake Forest

Follow the country road to Durley, passing a telephone box and a footpath sign for St Katharines on the right. The road cuts through a gently rolling parkland landscape. Walk down to the Column Ride and on the right you can see Tottenham House in the distance. The precise route of the Column Ride can be seen here, and very impressive it is. Turn left and follow the wide grassy ride, which is a permitted path. The monument can be seen ahead.

5. On reaching it, pause and enjoy this lovely woodland setting before beginning the next stage of the walk. Line up with the column and maintain the same direction as before, crossing over the forest track. Pass a barrier and go straight ahead. Roe and fallow deer may be seen among the trees. Continue through the woodland for about a mile and about 100 yards before reaching the A346, bear right to join a vague path. On reaching a firm track, turn left to the main road. Look for the old stone mile sign in the hedge – 'To Tottenham House, 2 miles, 3 furlongs and 143 yards. To Marlborough Town Hall, 2 miles, 7 furlongs and 70 yards'. Cross the road to join a narrow path opposite. Follow the path as it curves left to reach the road.

Keep right and follow the lane between trees, later passing a sign for the Royal Oak at Wootton Rivers. The road bends left and passes the remains of two railway tracks – one of which was a branch line serving Marlborough College. Extra trains were laid on for special events and other occasions during term time. Services operated until the 1960s.

6. Turn off at the next right-hand bridleway (left if you are walking the shorter route), Mud Lane, and take care along here in all seasons – in summer the path can be clogged with thick vegetation and at any time of the year it can get very wet and muddy. Keep going until you reach a prominent crossroads under some trees. Turn left and follow the wide track which drops down gently to reach the road. Go straight on towards Wootton Rivers. Pass the Royal Oak and return to the car park.

PLACE OF INTEREST NEARBY
Savernake Forest consists of more than 2,000 acres and was once a medieval hunting ground. Many walks and rides radiate out from the Grand Avenue, a magnificent 4-mile drive lined with stately beech and oak trees and designed by 'Capability' Brown in the 18th century. Henry VIII courted Jane Seymour here.

WALK 11

PEWSEY WHARF AND
THE GIANT'S GRAVE

A magnificent walk combining the gentle farming country of the Vale of Pewsey with the spectacular high ground of Martinsell Hill. From the top the views over Wiltshire are truly breathtaking. The route begins and ends on the towpath of the Kennet and Avon Canal.

The Kennet and Avon Canal near Pewsey

Pewsey Wharf was built to serve the village of Pewsey but it was never a great commercial success, eclipsed by other more profitable wharves on the Kennet and Avon Canal. The main building was intended to house the wharfinger – owner or keeper of the wharf – and the site remains much the same today as it was in the heyday of the canal era.

The village of Pewsey lies a short distance to the south of the wharf and contains various half-timbered houses and thatched cottages. But it is not just the village and the canal that make this an attractive part of Wiltshire – this is where rolling downland and spectacular scarp scenery give way to the delightful Vale of Pewsey, renowned for its low-lying clay landscape and described by the writer William Cobbett as 'my land of promise'.

Starting off eastwards along the Kennet and Avon towpath, the walk then heads to the high country, and up above the canal it reaches one of Wiltshire's most cherished landmarks – the Giant's Grave on Martinsell Hill. The 822 ft summit is chiefly associated with a charming legend which claims that anyone who runs along this unchambered long barrow seven times will wake the sleeping giant.

The French Horn by Pewsey Wharf is a delightful pub with an interesting history. During the Napoleonic War, French POWs, while building this stretch of the canal, were summoned to eat at this attractive inn by a French horn. Food is served every day and light fare might include sandwiches, fishcakes, salads, soup and ploughman's lunches. Wadworth 6X and IPA feature among the real ales and the pub has a popular beer garden. Telephone: 01672 562443.

- **HOW TO GET THERE:** Pewsey lies on the A345 between Marlborough and Salisbury. Pewsey Wharf is about ½ mile to the north of the railway station, just off the main road.
- **PARKING:** There is a free car park at Pewsey Wharf.
- **LENGTH OF THE WALK:** 6 miles. Map: OS Landranger 173 Swindon and Devizes (GR 157611).

THE WALK

1. Follow the towpath, keeping the canal on the left, and look towards the Giant's Grave and the spectacular ridge of hills across the Vale of Pewsey. Pass under a bridge and continue to the entrance to a wetland nature reserve, which is fed by springs bordering the Avon. The ground is constantly waterlogged and this offers ideal conditions for wildlife. Follow the towpath to the next bridge (112).

2. Pass under it and then bear immediately right up the bank to a gate. Turn right, cross the canal and head up the lane. Martinsell Hill dominates the skyline on this stretch of the walk. Follow the lane towards the escarpment and you will see the outline of the Giant's Grave over to the left. Pass a turning on the right for New Mill and keep ahead on the bridlepath. When it bends left go straight on along a track by some dilapidated outbuildings and alongside power lines. Head for the slopes of the escarpment and the path, muddy after rain, becomes

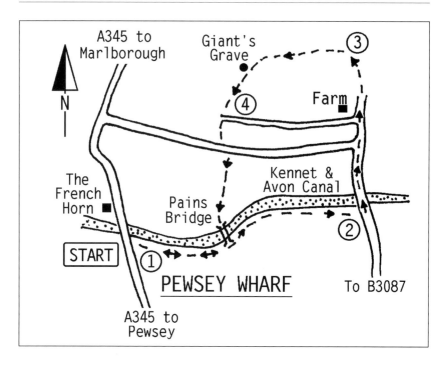

A345 to
Marlborough

Giant's
Grave

③

N

④

Farm

The
French
Horn ■

Pains
Bridge

Kennet &
Avon Canal

②

START ①

PEWSEY WHARF

To B3087

A345 to
Pewsey

progressively steeper. Follow the path to a galvanised gate and keep left. Complete the weary climb and at the top the views are tremendous.

3. Keep to the left of a gate, a stile and a sign for Martinsell Hill and veer round to the left. The Giant's Grave looms unexpectedly in front of you now. At the same time, the Vale of Pewsey and the glorious rolling carpet of the North Wiltshire Downs unfold before you. Walk along to the trig point and take care as you begin the steep descent; the path can get slippery. Keep the fence on the right and go down and round to the left to a stile in the bottom corner of the field. Glance back for a memorable view of the Giant's Grave rearing up among the hills. Walk down the field to a gate where there are bridleway and footpath signs.

4. Cross the track and follow the right edge of the field, making for the corner. Turn left at the road and go along to a sign for Inlands Farm. Follow the track between hedge and fence, pass a turning to the farm and continue on the track to Pains Bridge. Cross over and bear left

The Giant's Grave

down to the towpath. Go under the bridge and return to Pewsey Wharf.

PLACE OF INTEREST NEARBY

Knap Hill, to the north-west of Pewsey, is one of Wiltshire's lesser-known treasures and the site of a 4-acre Neolithic causewayed camp dating back to around 2760 BC. Nearby are the charming villages of Alton Barnes and Alton Priors. Alton is Anglo-Saxon for 'farm or village by the springs'. The springs can be seen very clearly bubbling away on the bed of a pretty little stream near the church of All Saints. The Alton Barnes White Horse was cut in 1812 and can be seen on the hillside.

DEVIZES AND THE 'GIANT'S VERTEBRAE'

Start this varied walk by exploring historic Devizes and its impressive buildings, then head for the Kennet and Avon Canal, following it west of the town. Leave the canal and head cross-country to the village of Rowde before returning to the Kennet and Avon. The last leg of the trail follows the waterway to the awe-inspiring Caen Hill flight of locks, one of its most famous landmarks.

The Caen Hill flight of locks

Before starting the walk, have a look at Devizes Wharf. Here the canalside has been much improved in recent years. Signs of industry have gone and today the towpath is part of an attractive scene enhanced by the former granary, which now houses a canal museum.

Devizes, one of Wiltshire's loveliest towns, is full of architectural delights. Round every corner and in every street, there is something to please the eye. Many of the famous listed buildings are to be found in the spacious Market Place and adjacent streets. In the late 1960s the centre of Devizes was used in the filming of the Thomas Hardy classic *Far from the Madding Crowd* and if it is one of your favourite films, you may well recognise some of the locations.

A stroll through Devizes is always a pleasure but it is the famous Caen Hill flight of locks, one of the great wonders of the canal era, which forms the main attraction of this fascinating town and country trail. Completed by John Rennie in 1810, in order to carry the Kennet and Avon Canal to a height of 237 ft, the flight consists of 29 locks in all, extending over 2 miles. The Caen Hill sequence of locks, 16 of them climbing up the hillside, has been described as the 'giant's vertebrae'. In the early days, the canal was so busy that gas lighting was installed in order that boats could negotiate the locks both day and night. Passage cost an extra shilling after dark. A record for ascending all 29 locks was achieved in 1991 when the crew of a narrowboat came through in 2 hours, 6 minutes and 51 seconds.

By the early 1950s the canal had fallen into decay, superseded by the road and rail network. When the Kennet and Avon was reopened by the Queen in 1990, one of the locks on the Caen Hill flight was named in her honour.

The George and Dragon at Rowde has been a pub since the 1500s. Beneath the old building are cellars where beer was once brewed. The imaginative menu offers some mouthwatering dishes – you may find, for example, Cornish crab salad, pheasant risotto and smoked salmon with scrambled eggs. The inn specialises in fresh fish from Cornwall. Preferably book to eat here as it can get very busy; there is no food on Sunday or Monday. Real ales include Wadworth 6X and several locally brewed guest beers. Telephone: 01380 723053. Alternatively, wait until you get back to Devizes before stopping for refreshments. There is a good choice of watering holes in the town. The Black Horse, on the canal towpath towards the end of the walk, is ideal for a stop. Telephone: 01380 723930.

- **HOW TO GET THERE:** Devizes lies to the north of Salisbury Plain, at the junction of the A360, the A361 and the A342. Make for New Park Street and turn off at the sign for the Wharf.
- **PARKING:** There is a car park at Devizes Wharf, where the walk begins.
- **LENGTH OF THE WALK:** 6 miles. Map: OS Landranger 173 Swindon and Devizes (GR 005617).

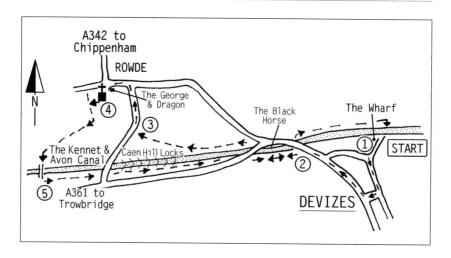

THE WALK

1. Before starting the walk, visit the Kennet and Avon Canal Museum by the car park and learn about this fascinating and historic waterway. Keep to the right of the premises of Devizes Angling Association and the Canal Bookshop and turn right into Couch Lane. Bear left at the next junction and pass Brownston House, which dates back to 1720 and is Grade I listed. Turn right at the pedestrian crossing and either go through the car park by the Market Hall or take the left-hand parallel route through a pedestrianised street known as The Brittox. Both routes lead to the spacious Market Place. Here, it is worth pausing for a moment or two to survey the jewel in the town's glittering crown.

The Bear Hotel and the Corn Exchange are among the most striking buildings and at the centre lies the splendid 1814 cross. One inscription reads: 'Erected by Henry, Viscount Sidmouth, as a memorial of his grateful attachment to the borough of Devizes, of which he has been recorder thirty years and of which he was six times unanimously chosen a representative in parliament. Anno Domini 1814.' The other inscription recalls the intriguing tale of Ruth Pierce who asked Heaven to strike her down dead if she lied during a disagreement over money at the local market. According to the inscription 'she instantly fell and expired'.

Walk along the street towards the towering red-brick façade of the Wadworth Brewery, passing the town's old cinema on the right. Continue ahead at the roundabout and don't be fooled into thinking there is a pub ahead. A familiar-looking inn sign, depicting the brewery building, can be seen attached to the side of the building but this is part of the brewery complex and most definitely is not a pub! Turn right at the sign – 'Caen Hill Locks via subway' – and join the towpath.

2. Pass under the main road and almost at once you sense the peace and tranquillity of the countryside as the sounds of Devizes begin to fade into the distance. Pass Maton Lock and follow the broad path beside the Kennet and Avon Canal. On approaching the next road bridge, veer slightly left away from the towpath for a few yards before turning right to cross the bridge. Turn immediately left to join a tarmac drive and keep right at the entrance to the Kennet and Avon Canal Maintenance Depot. Pass a sign 'Devizes welcomes you' and follow the drive ahead, curving to the right in due course. Glancing to the right reveals an impressive view of Roundway Hill, the setting for a famous Civil War battle in 1643.

3. Follow the drive to the road, turn right and follow the pavement and parallel path to the outskirts of Rowde. Walk along to the Cross Keys, turn left at the T junction and head through the village. Pass the George and Dragon and go straight on as the road bends right. Turn left immediately beyond the newsagents and follow the sheltered path to Rowde church. Go through the churchyard to the far boundary, keeping the church on your left, and exit to the road.

4. Turn right and walk through the housing estate; as the road bends right, turn left to join a track running between hedgerows. Follow it round to the right by a hard tennis court and some allotments and soon the track narrows to a path which can become quite thick with lush vegetation in summer. Pass a stile on the right and follow the path to a field. Cross the stile and bear immediately right along the field boundary. Make for the field corner which can be wet and muddy at times. Look for a stile here and cross into the woodland. After a few yards you reach a junction with a disused railway track, though it is hard to recognise today. The line, which closed in 1966, ran from Patney through Devizes to Holt and connected two mainline sections. Turn left and follow the old line to a lock on the Kennet and Avon Canal.

5. Cross the bridge by the lock gates and bear left. Follow the towpath towards Devizes and beyond the next road bridge the Caen Hill flight comes into view. Keep alongside it and further up you reach the lock named after the Queen. On this stretch, too, is a little bridge leading to

The canal at Devizes

Lock Cottage Tearooms where teas and ice creams are available. Continue on the towpath as far as the A361; if you are in need of a little sustenance, cross the bridge and make for the Black Horse. Retrace your steps to the bridge and continue on the towpath towards Devizes town centre. Go under the subway, leave the towpath to cross the road bridge and join the northern bank of the canal. Note the Artichoke pub along the road; this Wadworth house has been restored in recent years and is the closest pub to the brewery site just a few hundred yards away. Follow the towpath along to the next bridge, cross it and return to the car park.

PLACES OF INTEREST NEARBY

The *Kennet and Avon Canal Museum* near the start of the walk can be contacted on 01380 721279 for details of opening times. The *Devizes Visitor Centre* in the Market Square is well worth a visit, tracing the story of a town steeped in history and legend. Telephone: 01380 729408. The *Wiltshire Heritage Museum* in Long Street includes prehistoric collections of international renown from local landmark sites. Telephone: 01380 727369.

BRADFORD-ON-AVON: A CANAL AND TWO RIVERS WALK

Virtually every precious ingredient of our ever changing countryside is included on this glorious walk from Bradford-on-Avon west to Avoncliff Aqueduct and Iford. The river scenery by the Avon and the Frome is stunning, and for good measure there is a wonderful manor house with a dazzling garden open in the summer. If you're lucky, you might spot a grey wagtail or even a kingfisher.

The Avon

A lazy meandering river and acres of mellow local stone as far as the eye can see make Bradford-on-Avon, meaning 'broad ford', one of Wiltshire's loveliest towns. Close to the county's western boundary, Bradford-on-Avon straddles the river on the southern edge of the Cotswolds.

You can see at a glance that the town is hilly; rows of elegant terraced houses and an assortment of ancient stone weavers' cottages rise dramatically above the main river bridge, which is Bradford-on-Avon's focal point. Two of its 13th century arches survive although the lock-up was added during the 17th century when the bridge was widened.

For 600 years the town played a key role in the manufacture of wool and cloth and this tradition only ceased at the beginning of the 20th century. Fortunately, its architectural heritage is fiercely protected and local residents ensure that any building work is closely scrutinised to ensure that the town's charm, character and unique beauty remain intact.

One of Bradford-on-Avon's most historic landmarks is the Saxon church of St Laurence which dates from about AD 700. Tall and narrow with small windows, it was abandoned for centuries until Canon Jones, a noted historian, rediscovered it in 1856 and recognised it as a late Saxon building. Don't miss the carved angels high up on the east wall of the nave.

Iford Manor has a striking classical front which was added around 1730 by William Chanler, a salter and mill-owner from Bradford-on-Avon. Parts of the house date from around 1500 with extensions during the reign of Elizabeth I. When the architect Harold Peto acquired the house in 1899, it was in a poor state of repair. Peto was particularly interested in horticulture and landscape design and he set about transforming Iford's garden into a work of art. The results of his labours can be viewed on certain days during the summer months.

Just a few yards from the walk, the Inn at Freshford is a traditional country inn with large gardens and a pretty setting. Food is served every day and the specials board changes weekly. There are children's meals too. Telephone: 01225 722250.

- **HOW TO GET THERE:** Bradford-on-Avon is located on the A363 Bath to Trowbridge road.
- **PARKING:** The walk starts at the spacious car park by the railway station on the south side of the Avon, near the bridge.
- **LENGTH OF THE WALK:** 7 miles. Map: OS Landranger 173 Swindon and Devizes and 172 Bristol and Bath (GR 825607).

THE WALK

1. Leave the station car park by keeping the railway line on your left. Follow the path under the bridge and keep alongside the bank of the Avon. Cut across the grass and look back for a memorable view of

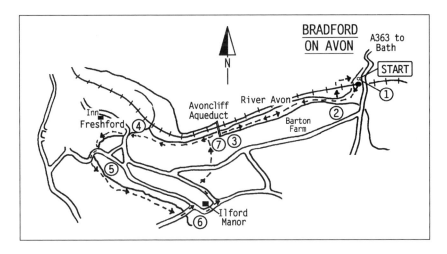

Bradford-on-Avon up on the hillside. Along here an authentic packhorse bridge can be seen spanning the river. Follow the tarmac path through Barton Farm Country Park and make for a map with information about the park. Branch off to the left here to visit the 14th century tithe barn, noted for its superb roof structure. On a sunny day, it is pleasantly dark and cool inside.

2. Return to the map, turn left and continue along the park path. Keep the river on your right and cut between wood, scrub and grassland habitats. Pass a seat and information panel and veer half right to join the lower path here. Follow the path by the water's edge, cut through the trees and cross pretty meadows. Eventually the path becomes enclosed again by vegetation; the sound of nearby trains and rushing water is also clearly audible along here.

3. Approach the weir at Avoncliff, go up the steps here and turn right, following the Kennet and Avon Canal towpath. Soon it bends right by some pretty cottages to reach the 110 yard long Avoncliff Aqueduct, constructed in 1798. On the right is a pub, the Cross Guns. Turn left as you approach the pub and pass under the stone structure. Take the drive alongside the houses and pass an old workhouse which has recently been converted into luxury apartments. As the track bends left, go straight on through a wrought iron kissing gate into the trees. Follow the path to a second gate and continue ahead across an elongated field with a pillbox seen over to the right. Make for another wrought iron gate in the trees and follow the woodland path to a meadow. Cross it to a kissing gate by the ancient stone road bridge over the Frome.

4. With the Inn at Freshford just a few paces to the right, turn left and follow the lane along to a stile and footpath sign on the right. Cross the field, keeping to the left of a pillbox, and look for a stile in the boundary ahead. Go across the next field to a stile by the road. Turn right here and follow the lane as it bends left. At this stage of the walk, you are treated to a delightful view of the River Frome. Follow the lane by the water and then up through the trees to a sign for Dunkirk Mill Cottage. Turn left to join a bridleway here and follow the track to a large house on the right. Bear left opposite the entrance to join a footpath. Looking down into the valley reveals a charming view of the Frome and a weir. Make for a gate and drop down the grassy path to a track, turning left for a few steps to the entrance to Whistlers Hollow.

5. Keep right at the fork and follow the field path to a gate. Head down through the woodland to a second gate and follow the edge of the watermeadow with trees on the right. Aim for a stile in the corner, turn left and walk along to Iford Manor. This is a stunning setting, with the beautiful manor house overlooking the Frome. Turn right in front of the house and follow the narrow lane, Iford Hill, as it rises quite steeply between walls. The ascent becomes more demanding further up.

6. Head for the junction and turn left. Follow the road all the way to a sign on the right for Upper Westwood. The path broadens out further on and soon reaches the road. Turn right in Westwood, then left between houses after about 30 yards to join a track. Cross a stile by a gate and descend the hillslope with glorious views down into the valley. Rolling hills and wooded slopes dominate this enchanting scenic landscape. Make for the bottom right corner of the field, cross a stile into the woodland, go down the steps and turn sharp left. Follow the path round to the right and down to a stile on the edge of the woodland. Head down the field to a gate in the right corner. Follow the track down the slope, round to the right and along to Avoncliff Aqueduct.

7. Turn right by the Cross Guns and join the canal towpath. Follow it until you reach a wooden footbridge. Here you have a choice of routes which both meet up further on; the towpath and a lower path running down between the trees and through Barton Farm Country Park. Assuming you follow the latter, cut through the park and keep the tithe barn on the right. Then turn left across the packhorse bridge, cross the railway to Barton Orchard and follow the sign for the Saxon church. Pass The Chantry before reaching the medieval church of Holy Trinity on the right and the Saxon church of St Laurence on the left. Cross the footbridge beyond it, go through the car park to the road, turn right and right again for the station car park.

PLACES OF INTEREST NEARBY

The gardens of *Iford Manor* are open on Sunday during April and October between 2 pm and 5 pm, and from May until September daily between 2 pm and 5 pm, except Monday and Friday. Home-made teas are available from May to August at weekends and on bank holidays. The gardens are also open on Easter Monday. Telephone: 01225 863146.

The *Bradford-on-Avon Museum* in Bridge Street includes aspects of the natural and historical heritage of the town. One of its main features is a pharmacy shop which stood for more than 100 years in Bradford-on-Avon before being removed and painstakingly rebuilt here. Telephone: 01225 863280.

Avoncliff Aqueduct

HEYTESBURY: A WALK BY THE WYLYE
❧

A delightful walk taking you along the banks of the River Wylye to the villages of Upton Lovell and Corton. The Wylye, one of Wiltshire's lesser-known rivers, threads its way through some of the loveliest scenery in the county.

The River Wylye

Anyone familiar with the history of Heytesbury will tell you that during the 20th century the village became closely identified with one man – the First World War poet Siegfried Sassoon who died in 1967. After surviving the horrors of war, Sassoon made his home at Heytesbury. Like many officers of his generation, he was stationed in this area for training on Salisbury Plain and during his time here he grew to love Wiltshire's dramatic views and wide horizons. It was his fondness for this spacious downland country that inspired him to buy Heytesbury House in the late 1920s.

As well as being a poet, Sassoon was also a novelist and autobiographer, but it is his account of the Great War in verse for which most people remember him. Together with Wilfrid Owen, Edmund Blunden, Ivor Gurney and many others, Sassoon managed to evoke vivid, haunting images of bloodshed and brutality on the battlefields of Europe. Above all, his work illustrates the sheer futility of war.

Heytesbury was once a borough noted for sheep rearing. It became the main wool warehouse of the Hungerford family who were granted the right to hold fairs and markets. Heytesbury's close proximity to the River Wylye attracted cloth mills along its course but ambitious plans to develop it into a thriving industrial centre the size of Warminster never materialised. When William Cobbett rode through Heytesbury in 1826 it was a rotten borough still returning its two members. 'What was formerly a considerable town is now but a very miserable affair,' he remarked. Borough status was lost in the Great Reform Act of 1832 and by 1932 the population had fallen from 1,412 to a mere 454.

The Red Lion in Heytesbury is a welcoming inn offering a range of sandwiches and ploughman's lunches as well as a variety of more substantial fare, including pies, fish and steak. Home-cooked food is served every day and the pub has a popular riverside beer garden. Bass and Butcombe ale feature among the beers and there are usually three lagers available. The pub also has accommodation available. Telephone: 01985 840315.

- **HOW TO GET THERE:** Heytesbury lies on the western edge of Salisbury Plain, just off the A36 Salisbury to Warminster and Bath road.
- **PARKING:** There is room to park in the main street of the village.
- **LENGTH OF THE WALK:** 5 miles. Map: OS Landranger 184 Salisbury and The Plain (GR 925425).

THE WALK

1. With your back to the Red Lion turn right and walk along the village street. Notice the variety of houses lining the road, distinguished by their different architectural styles. Pass the Angel Inn and when the road bends left, go straight on into Park Street. Follow the road to the point where it terminates, within sight of the A36, then join the tarmac path between grass and margins of vegetation.

2. Keep alongside the main road until you see some steps on the right. Take them and make for a wrought iron kissing gate. Follow the path across the fields and through woodland and soon you reach the bank

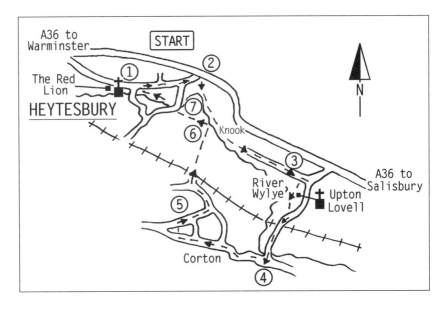

of the Wylye. Keep to the riverside path, ignore the wooden footbridge and continue on a cinder track beside the water. The river can now be seen curving away to the right. Keep ahead at the next junction, following a lane between houses and farm outbuildings. Pass through the gap to the left of several galvanised gates and continue on a clear path to skirt a field by its right-hand boundary. Go through another galvanised gate in the field corner and continue ahead on a narrow tarmac lane into the village of Upton Lovell.

3. Modern houses and cottages line the road and on the right is the Prince Leopold pub, dated 1878. Look for the GR letter box set in the wall by the telephone box. Follow the road until it bends left by a brick and stone wall. Go straight ahead by the Old Rectory on the right. Pass the quintessentially English church on the left, occupying a delightfully secluded spot beside the route of the walk. Curve left to join a drive and turn right at the road. Cross the railway and the river and turn right at the junction.

4. Follow the road towards Corton, taking care along here as there is occasional traffic. On reaching Foley's Cottage, turn right and go down several steps and along a path leading to the next road. Turn right and pass the Dove Inn.

5. Avoid the path on the right and pass Sundial House. When the road bends left, turn right at the 'no through road' sign by a bungalow. Pass Sundial Farm and go under the railway line. Avoid a wide track on the right and continue ahead on a grassy path between trees and hedgerows. Cross the little stream via the footbridge and continue. This stretch of the walk can get overgrown with cow parsley in the summer months. Continue to a footbridge and a stile. Cross the field to another tributary, followed almost immediately by the Wylye. Don't cross the river; instead turn left immediately before the footbridge.

6. Avoid the path alongside the Wylye, cross a track and head over the field, keeping the boundary on your left. Exit in the corner and turn right to follow an enclosed path. Cross a track and now thatched cottages and a mill are visible. At the next road, by the Wylye, turn right to cross the river and then bear immediately left through a kissing gate.

7. Follow the riverbank and pass through several kissing gates. Join a drive, pass a seat on the left and on reaching the next junction, keep left along Mill Street. Carry on along the lane and now you can see Heytesbury church ahead. Cross the road into the churchyard and return to the centre of the village.

PLACE OF INTEREST NEARBY

For something a little different, try walking all or part of the *Imber Range Path*, a 30-mile circular walk following the outer boundary of the military firing and training area on Salisbury Plain. From the path you are treated to superb views of west Wiltshire and when visibility is good you can see up to 15 miles or more. Ironically, in this overcrowded country of ours, Salisbury Plain is one of the least populated tracts of land in the south of England.

AMESBURY: ALONG THE AVON
❧❀❧

This spectacular downland walk begins in the little Wiltshire town of Amesbury, a stone's throw from the more famous Stonehenge, and then makes for breezy, uncluttered country to the south of it. On the return leg, the walk runs parallel to the pretty waters of the Avon. If you are feeling energetic, make a whole day of it and join this route to walk 16, using the unrestricted all day car park in Recreation Road at point 1.

The Avon at Amesbury

Amesbury lies along the eastern edge of Salisbury Plain and is renowned in some quarters for its Arthurian associations. It appears King Arthur may have harboured a fondness for the area. There are claims, too, that the name Amesbury comes from Ambrosius Aurelianus, a Roman Briton who happened to be the uncle of King Arthur. After the King's death, in the 6th century, it is said that Queen Guinevere sought refuge in the Wessex region, probably fleeing to an abbey.

Amesbury Abbey, rebuilt in the mid-19th century and now a nursing home, stands on the site of the original abbey which was constructed in AD 979. The present house, which has a colonnaded front raised on five arches, was built by Thomas Hopper for Sir Edward Antrobus, owner of the Stonehenge estate. The Avon flows prettily through its parkland.

Amesbury's ancient church was built by the Saxons and remodelled by the Normans. The Norman font was rescued from beneath the floor and set on a carved base 500 years old. But the church we see today is essentially 13th century, with 15th and 16th century roofs, striking tracery and carved bosses. The church is also noted for one rather unusual feature – a head carved into the aisle roof depicting Henry VIII as a cherub.

The Kings Arms, opposite the Church Street car park, offers hot and cold meals and traditional ales. There is a restaurant at the rear. Typical pub fare features ploughman's lunches, jacket potatoes, and sandwiches – including cheese, ham, prawn and bacon. Telephone: 01980 626662. The Friar Tuck café in the centre of Amesbury serves food, tea and coffee all day.

- **HOW TO GET THERE:** Amesbury is 8 miles north of Salisbury and 20 miles south of Marlborough, at the junction of the A303 and the A345.
- **PARKING:** Amesbury has a short stay car park in Church Street, near the Antrobus Arms. Alternatively, park at the larger car park on the A345, near the old Plaza Cinema, or use the recreation ground car park and start the walk there.
- **LENGTH OF THE WALK:** 4 miles. Map: OS Landranger 184 Salisbury and The Plain (GR 153415).

THE WALK

1. From the car park in Church Street turn right and walk along to the Avon. Just beyond it, where the road bends right by the junction with Recreation Road, bear left by a thatched cottage. Follow the track, go through a kissing gate and pass the cemetery. When the track bends right, go straight on along the grassy track, joining the obvious path here. Soon it runs alongside the river and over to the left along this stretch are good views towards Amesbury. Pass through a gate to a weir and continue on the path as it bends left and then right to reach a junction.

73

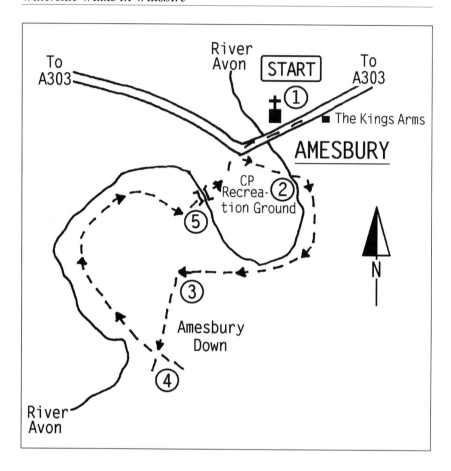

2. Turn right here by South Mill and follow the track through the trees, keeping the river close by on the right. When the track forks, keep left on the bridleway and begin a moderate climb. Follow the grassy track and merge with a farm access track. Pausing for a few moments reveals memorable views back towards Amesbury. Keep on the track until you reach an obvious junction with some barns and outbuildings ahead.

3. Turn left here and join a bridleway. Follow the track, making for a galvanised gate and a wrought iron kissing gate. The bridleway goes straight on; the footpath turns right. Bear right here and follow the path along the field edge to the corner where there is a gate. (Turn left here to link up with route 16 at point 5, walk through Great Durnford to Lake, then eventually return to this junction and continue at point 4.)

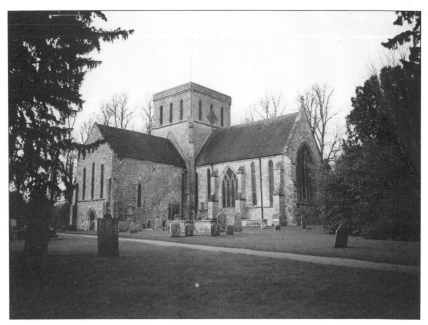

Amesbury church

4. Go through the gate, follow the field edge and continue for some time along the boundary. Cross several fields, keeping trees and bushes to your left. Pass over a track further on and continue ahead along the field perimeter. Eventually you reach a pair of semi-detached cottages; turn left at the sign for Amesbury (½ mile).

5. Follow the riverside path over two footbridges and along to the recreation ground. Follow the lane down to the road and go straight on to return to the car park in Church Street.

PLACES OF INTEREST NEARBY
Stonehenge is a World Heritage Site of unique importance and interest, surrounded by the remains of ceremonial and domestic structures. The site is to the west of Amesbury, at the junction of the A344 and the A303. Telephone: 01980 624715.

The massive Iron Age hillfort of *Old Sarum* near Salisbury was used by the Romans, Saxons and Normans and contains the ruins of a castle, cathedral and Bishop's Palace. For more information call 01722 335398.

WALK 16

GREAT DURNFORD: AMBLING
THROUGH THE WOODFORD VALLEY

The Woodford valley, threaded by the Avon, extends from Amesbury to Salisbury where it becomes the Avon valley. Great Durnford's unspoilt rural setting has to be one of the loveliest in the whole of Wiltshire, and quite unforgettable when the sun is dancing on the river, bathing the watermeadows and the surrounding pastures in a warm golden glow. Appropriately, the only real way to explore the Woodford valley and appreciate its gentle beauty is on foot. This walk and route 15 at Amesbury are so close together, they can be joined to make a spectacular 10-mile hike.

Great Durnford village

Great Durnford is the quintessential English village. With its impressive Norman church, picturesque thatched cottages, flower-filled gardens, handsome manor house and welcoming pub, it has everything you would expect to find in such a place.

76

St Andrew's church is well worth closer inspection. Its north and south doorways both have the zigzag pattern outside and high rounded arches on the inside. There is further evidence of zigzag work around the chancel arch. In the chancel itself is a monument to Edward Younge whose father married into the Tropenell family of Monkton Farleigh near Bath and later inherited the manor of Little Durnford. Originally known as Hungerford Magna, Great Durnford means 'hidden ford'.

Lake House dates from the end of the 16th century and is characterised by its flint and stone chequer elevations, with an assortment of small pointed gables. The house, built for the clothier George Duke, is one of the finest in the area and has a distinctly Elizabethan look about it even though it was extensively restored following a fire in 1912. Lake House belonged to the Duke family for nine generations.

William Cobbett visited this part of Wiltshire in 1826 and was gravely concerned by the plight of the farm labourer. He expressed his 'deep shame, as an Englishman, at beholding the general extreme poverty of those who cause this vale to produce such quantities of food and raiment'. One hundred and seventy five years later, there is still widespread rural deprivation, with many farmers struggling to make a living.

The Black Horse at Great Durnford is a traditional country pub offering a range of main meals and snacks, including baguettes, ploughman's lunches and soup. There is bed and breakfast, a beer garden and a Sunday roast. Telephone: 01722 782270.

- **HOW TO GET THERE:** Great Durnford is north of Salisbury, between the A360 and the A345. From Amesbury follow the road south into the Woodford valley. From Salisbury take the A345 and follow the signs for Great Durnford.
- **PARKING:** You should be able to leave your car in the main street or in the vicinity of the church.
- **LENGTH OF THE WALK:** 6 miles. Map: OS Landranger 184 Salisbury and The Plain (GR 136383).

THE WALK

1. Keep the church on your right and walk along the main street through the village. Pass a bridleway and a turning for the Winterbournes on the left; continue through Great Durnford towards Netton and Woodford. Pass the Black Horse and a few paces beyond it turn right, signposted to Durnford Mill.

2. Cut between poplar trees and follow the track, keeping to the right of the mill. Cross the Avon at the weir and continue to the next bridge. Avoid a path on the left and continue, passing alongside trees and sloping fields. On reaching the road at Lake, cross over to a stile and walk ahead. On the right is Lake House.

3. Follow the path over this elevated ground, with good views across the valley. A mixture of beech and oak trees adds to the charming scene. Cross a stile, emerge from the trees and follow the field edge down to Lake Bottom. Turn left at the junction and follow the byway. Keep to the grassy track and now the walk cuts through a remote downland landscape, with the moan of the breeze and the distant thud of artillery fire on Salisbury Plain the only sounds to break the soothing silence. Keep right at the next fork, pass some paddocks and approach Springbottom Farm.

4. If you want to extend the walk and visit Stonehenge (a 3-mile return detour), keep left at this point and follow the track as it runs north. Otherwise, turn sharp right at the farm, pass the outbuildings and walk along the tarmac drive. When it curves right, join the parallel path on the left of it, running through the trees. This stretch of the walk is very pleasant on a hot summer day. From the higher ground there are glimpses of Stonehenge in the distance. Bear left at the road and follow it to a postbox by some houses. Turn right here between brick pillars and wrought iron gates. Follow the drive and look for a stile on the left, just before the house. Take the path across the field, keeping the house and thatched or 'cob' walling on the right. Head for the river, crossing it at the footbridge. The path to Great Durnford is to the right. (If you want to joint this route to walk 15, turn left here, then head for a gate and the field boundary at point 4 of the Amesbury circuit. Follow the path to the town and eventually return to this junction.)

5. Follow the path as it begins to ascend, keeping to the field edge. Bear right through a gate at the top into the next field. Turn left and follow the boundary; there are glorious views of the valley at this stage of the walk. Pass over a bridleway track and continue along the field edge. Make for the corner and go through a galvanised gate. Walk ahead, following the permitted path through the vegetation. Aim for a track and skirt the woodland edge. Pass through the trees and head for the road. Keep right here and follow the lane back to the centre of

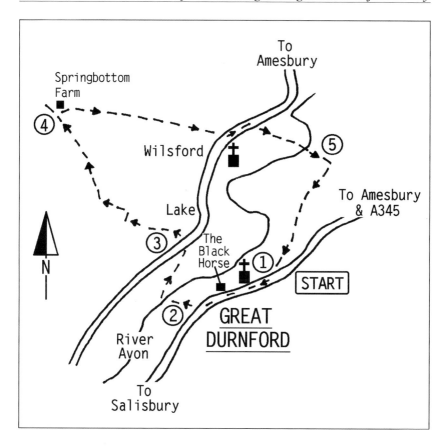

Great Durnford. Over to the left lie the remains of Ogbury Camp, an extensive Iron Age hillfort.

PLACE OF INTEREST NEARBY

Heale House Gardens and Plant Centre, just to the south of Great Durnford, comprise 8 acres of beautiful gardens in a formal setting of mellow stonework and clipped hedges. There are delightful walks here through the different seasons, and unusual plants, including many growing in the garden, can be bought in the specialist Plant Centre. Heale House is well known in Wiltshire for sheltering Charles II after the Battle of Worcester in 1651. He even found time, so it is said, to visit Stonehenge while he was here! The house is not open to the public. For more information about the gardens and plant centre call 01722 782504.

GREAT WISHFORD AND STAPLEFORD: WHERE TWO RIVERS MEET

This superb walk offers a fine mix of downland and valley scenery. From the delightful village of Great Wishford it follows a section of the Monarch's Way across remote open country, eventually descending the valley slopes to reach the village of Stapleford. The walk heads for the River Till, following it to its confluence with the Wylye; the return leg offers views over miles of picturesque countryside as it follows the lush riverbank.

The meandering Wylye

Mention the village of Great Wishford and most people immediately associate it with one date in the calendar – 29th May. This is Oak Apple Day when an old custom, which has its origins in pre-Christian tree worship, permits the villagers to gather fallen and dead wood from nearby Grovely Wood. The custom still includes a ritual ceremony which involves residents processing to Salisbury Cathedral where, at the steps of the high altar, they proclaim their rights, chanting 'Grovely! Grovely! and all Grovely! Unity is strength.'

Before beginning the walk have a look at the splendid church of St Giles. Inside you can see the oldest known manual fire engine, purchased by the churchwardens in 1728. They paid the princely sum of thirty-three pounds and three shillings for it! The fire engine is a horse-drawn four-wheel type of wooden construction. Over the years the church has benefited from a considerable amount of restoration work, including major improvements to the tower. A sixth bell was added in 1977. In 1863/4 the church was largely rebuilt by T. H. Wyatt, the architect for Wilton parish church and a relative of James Wyatt who restored Salisbury Cathedral.

In the wall outside the church you can pick out the bread stones – a fascinating local feature. These tablets indicate the price of a gallon of bread from the Napoleonic Wars onwards. At the start of the 19th century, England and France were at loggerheads; the French blockaded this country and, as a result, prices soared. The parish of Great Wishford was badly hit, with villagers having to pay 8d more for their bread than neighbouring communities. In an effort to reassure residents that the asking price was genuine, the local baker recorded his price in stone in the churchyard wall and the tradition has been maintained ever since. To celebrate the Millennium and the bicentenary of the first bread stone, a further stone was added by the council in 2000, with the price recorded as £3.72p per gallon. The gallon measurement was used in a local bakery until its closure in 1982.

The Royal Oak in Great Wishford caters for all tastes and offers a wide range of dishes. Steaks, pies and fish are available; for something lighter, choose from a selection of jacket potatoes, baguettes and ploughman's. There is also a popular Sunday carvery. Food is served every day and Ringwood and Hop Back feature among the real ales. Telephone: 01722 790079.

- **HOW TO GET THERE:** Great Wishford lies just off the A36 between Salisbury and Warminster. Turn off westwards at Stoford.
- **PARKING:** There is usually room to park in South Street, near the church.
- **LENGTH OF THE WALK:** 5 miles. Map: OS Landranger 184 Salisbury and The Plain (GR 081353).

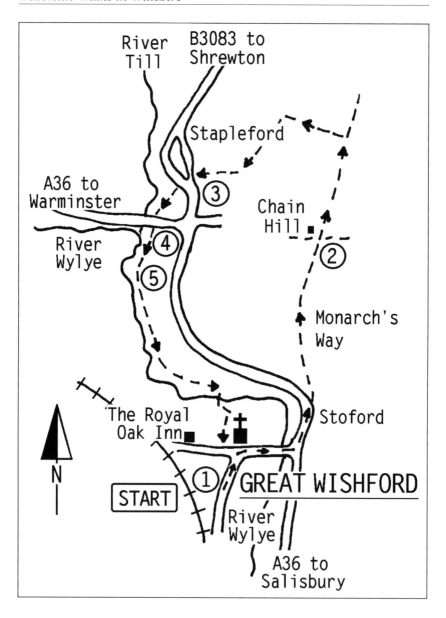

THE WALK

1. From South Street walk along to the church. Keep St Giles' on your left and look for the bread stones in the wall by the junction. Turn right into West Street and walk along to the A36, crossing the Wylye just before the junction. Bear left and pass the Swan Inn. As the road begins to curve left by the 40-mile speed signs, veer off to the right and go up the slope, following the unsurfaced track through the trees to a field. This is part of the Monarch's Way – the long-distance trail which follows Charles II's escape route after the Battle of Worcester in 1651. Follow the trail towards Chain Hill and if you glance back down over the valley, you can identify the trees of Grovely Wood in the distance.

2. On reaching a barn at the junction with Chain Drove, go straight on to the next junction. At this point we part company with the Monarch's Way as it bears right here. We continue ahead. Pass alongside conifer plantations and a few hundred yards beyond the woodland, turn left, following the downland track as it curves left a little further on. After ½ mile or so, the track swings right and down below, nestling in the valley, are the houses of Stapleford. The name means a marked crossing point and the village is one of seven in the country bearing this name. Follow the track down through the trees to the road.

3. At this stage of the walk, it's worth making a short detour in order to rest and relax for a few minutes – especially on a hot day when there is little shade from the burning sun. Turn right and head down to the

Great Wishford church

junction by Over Street, go through the gate here and look for a couple of seats where you can sit and admire the delightful riverside scene. The River Till flows through Stapleford, on its way to meet the Wylye immediately to the south of the village. Walk back up Butts Hill and follow the lane down to the next junction. Cross the B3083 and join a bridleway. Approach Seymour Cottage and veer to the left of it. Keep right at the fork and follow the path between meadows and pastures to a kissing gate.

4. Cross the A36, turn right and walk along the road for a short distance to the Pelican Inn, situated on the banks of the Till. There has been a bridge over the river here for 350 years. Turn left by the bridge and follow the path alongside the Till. Cross several stiles to a footbridge and go diagonally across the meadow towards a further stile. Don't cross it; instead, keep the river (now the Wylye) and the fence on your right. Make for a footbridge and then cross the meadow, still keeping the river on your right. Look for a stile ahead as the river sweeps away to the right.

5. Walk alongside trees and bushes, cross a stile and then head straight across the pasture to rejoin the riverbank. Keep alongside the Wylye, pass a bridge and gate and continue to two stiles. The buildings of Little Wishford are seen along this stretch of the riverbank. Over to the right is the route of a railway line and passing trains may catch you by surprise here. Continue by the Wylye and pass a picturesque thatched cottage over on the opposite bank. Head for a stile and footbridge and cross the river at this point. Swing left towards some farm outbuildings and aim for the stile to the right of them. Turn right and follow the drive to the road at Great Wishford. This is North Street and the Royal Oak is to the right. To finish the walk, turn left and then veer right as you approach the church, returning to South Street where the walk began.

PLACE OF INTEREST NEARBY

Originally a 9th century nunnery, *Wilton House*, south of Great Wishford, includes Inigo Jones state rooms, a renowned art collection, modern interpretative displays and 21 acres of landscaped parkland. Telephone: 01722 746729.

FONTHILL'S ELEGANT PARKLAND: A LAKESIDE WALK

Explore some of the prettiest countryside in this corner of Wiltshire on this superb woodland walk through Fonthill Park. The route begins in Fonthill Bishop and soon heads for the shores of a large, tree-fringed lake before cutting across lonely country to the remote settlement of Ridge. The walk is truly delightful but, with the possible exception of around the lake, don't be surprised if you don't meet anyone else along the way!

The lake at Fonthill Bishop

The vast Fonthill estate, in the unspoilt Nadder valley, recalls England's feudal system, weekend house parties and the heyday of the aristocracy. Explore the estate village of Fonthill Bishop and its neighbouring parkland and you will surely agree that even today it has that feel about it. Several hundred people live and are employed on this sprawling estate which is owned by the landowner Lord Margadale. Within its boundaries is a beautiful lake which was used in the summer of 2000 for the filming of Joanne Harris' novel, *Chocolat*. The film has a distinguished cast, with Judi Dench and Juliette Binoche among the main performers. During the making of the movie, a mock galleon was deliberately blown up on the lake and various changes were made to the surroundings. The walk passes through a splendid arched gateway attributed to Inigo Jones before reaching the water's edge.

Not far away to the west, though sadly not visible and not open to the public, are the remains of Fonthill Abbey, built in the late 18th century by William Beckford, the eccentric millionaire and author, and described by Pevsner as 'his great Gothic folly'. The scale of the plan was such that the Abbey tower was intended to be as high as St Paul's Cathedral.

Beckford built in a great hurry, employing 500 men to work day and night and keeping fires burning to prevent plaster and cement from freezing. He even entertained Nelson and Lady Hamilton here for three nights in 1800. During his time here, Beckford also established large plantations and built a 12 ft wall around the extensive parkland. However, in 1823, he abandoned the place and moved to Bath, his ambitious plans having proved too much. The Abbey collapsed several years later.

The Beckford Arms lies just off the route of the walk, close to the lake, by Fonthill Gifford church. Here you can enjoy light starters or snacks, including soup and baguettes. More substantial meals are served and there is a beer garden with a weeping ash as old as the pub itself. A range of real ales is available and lagers include Carlsberg and Stella Artois. Large groups are asked to book for food. The inn also has eight letting rooms. Telephone: 01747 870385.

- **HOW TO GET THERE:** Fonthill Bishop, near Hindon, is on the B3089, about 1 mile south of the A303.
- **PARKING:** There is room to park in the village, especially in the vicinity of the church.
- **LENGTH OF THE WALK:** 5 miles. Map: OS Landranger 184 Salisbury and The Plain (GR 935328).

THE WALK

1. Keep the church on your right and veer left just beyond the speed de-restriction sign (signposted to Tisbury). Follow the road through the arched gateway and over to the left is the lake set in elegant parkland

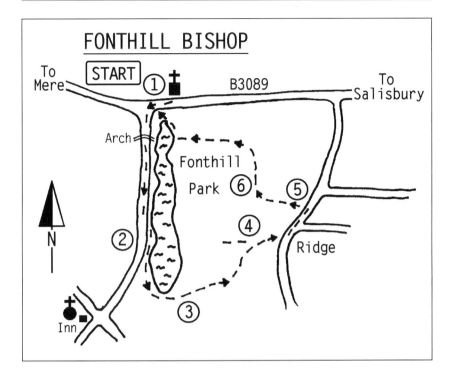

and enclosed by trees. Pass several turnings on the right and continue to a layby.

2. Make for the little gate at the far end and follow the path through the trees with the lake over to the left. Merge with a track running down from the right and head for a pair of double wooden gates and a single gate. Beyond them follow the track as it curves round the southern end of the lake, over the sluice. Veer right at the sign, then swing sharp left after about 50 yards, heading up the slope through the trees.

3. There are glimpses of the lake as you make the ascent. Pick your way through the trees and veer right at the fork, climbing steeply now. There are glorious views in all directions as you make for the corner of a field. Keep to its right boundary and looking back reveals glimpses of the spire of Fonthill Gifford church peeping through the trees. Head for the field corner, keep left and skirt the field with the woodland now on your right. Look for an opening on the right and follow the waymarked path through the trees, keeping to the edge of the woodland. Fonthill House can be seen across the paddocks, nestling among the trees. On reaching a track, bear left and walk along to the next junction.

4. Turn right and follow the tarmac drive through the trees to some white gateposts. Bear left here and walk along the lane. Go down the slope and ahead, nestling against the trees, are the rooftops of Ridge, a hamlet. Head up the hillside, passing a telephone box and a right-hand path, and swing left immediately before the junction at the top.

5. There is a wide gate here, with a single gate to the right of it. A bridleway sign is also seen. On reaching a fork, veer right and note the carpets of bluebells along here in spring. Follow the track through the trees and just before it bends right to a field, turn right and cut through a strip of woodland.

6. Continue on the track as it climbs quite steeply and soon you are treated to magnificent views across the isolated countryside that characterises this walk. Make for the crest of the hillside and here you can spot the lake which featured in the early stages of the route. In time the track curves to the right and gradually the rooftops of Fonthill Bishop loom into view. Walk through a yard enclosed by old stables converted into offices and then turn right to follow the drive to the road.

PLACES OF INTEREST NEARBY
Old Wardour Castle near Ansty, south of Tisbury, was wrecked by the Parliamentarians in 1643. The castle ruins occupy a picturesque lakeside setting and the site includes landscaped grounds with a striking rockwork grotto. Telephone: 01747 870487.

The landscaped gardens at *Stourhead*, owned by the National Trust, are among the finest in the country. The lakes, dating from 1448, temples, shrubs and rare trees feature in countless books, calendars and postcards. The Palladian mansion was built in the 1720s and the estate also includes Alfred's Tower, a famous folly built in 1772. Telephone: 01747 841152.

THE AVON, THE NADDER AND SALISBURY'S SOARING SPIRE

Starting at Harnham, on the outskirts of Salisbury, this easy, undemanding walk along the Nadder to Salisbury Cathedral offers an assortment of riches and scenic delights. By starting outside Salisbury, it avoids the problem of parking and yet takes you right to the heart of the city. Stroll by the Avon and visit the magnificent Close before beginning the return leg across the famous watermeadows.

The Old Mill Hotel

Sheltered by sweeping downland and located at the meeting point of four river valleys, Salisbury is one of Britain's loveliest cathedral cities. Few settings in this country match the beauty and elegance of the Cathedral and Close, and Constable's famous painting immortalises the stunning view of the spire, the tallest in England, from the nearby meadows – a classic, timeless picture.

Salisbury Cathedral was started in 1220 and completed around 1280, though the 404 ft spire was added in 1334. The Cloister and Chapter House, which contains a medieval frieze and an original 1215 Magna Carta, date back to 1280. The Cathedral is the only ecclesiastical building in England to be constructed throughout in the same Early English style and it stands today as a permanent testimony to the skill and ingenuity of medieval builders.

This site was chosen when Bishop Richard Poore abandoned the Norman cathedral on the fortified hill of Old Sarum because it lacked a proper water supply. The lush, level watermeadows on the lower ground were considered more suitable and the alternative site was called 'New Sarum'.

Thomas Hardy loved Salisbury – his two sisters trained as teachers here. 'The Close of Salisbury under the full summer moon on a windless night is as beautiful a scene as any I know in England or, for the matter of that, elsewhere,' he wrote. Salisbury was the inspiration for Melchester which appears in some of Hardy's works, including *Jude the Obscure*. In the book Jude worked as a stonemason on the Cathedral.

The Old Mill Hotel and Inn, passed at the end of the walk, dates back to 1135 and was converted in 1550 to Wiltshire's first paper mill when the Nadder was diverted to its present course under the building. Inside are cosy low-beamed bars and a restaurant serving lunch and dinner. Bar meals and snacks, including sandwiches and jacket potatoes, are available from Monday to Saturday. A set lunch is served on Sunday. Telephone: 01722 327517.

- **HOW TO GET THERE:** Harnham lies just to the south of Salisbury, on the A3094.
- **PARKING:** There is a small free car park off the A3094 at Harnham, opposite Saxon Road and close to a strip of green in the middle of the road. Alternatively, travel to Salisbury by train and begin the walk at the city railway station (at the end of point 3).
- **LENGTH OF THE WALK:** 4 miles. Map: OS Landranger 184 Salisbury and The Plain (GR 136291).

THE WALK

1. From the car park turn right and follow Harnham Road for a short distance. Veer right into Lower Street, passing the car park of St George's church on the left, and continue along the road. Avoid Town Path on the right and walk ahead along Middle Street. Pass the Old Mill House and the aptly named Constable Way and look for Middle Street

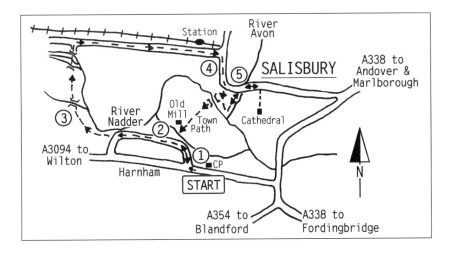

Meadow on the right, a native wildflower meadow between the houses of Harnham and the banks of the Nadder.

2. Leave the road at the meadow, bear left and follow its boundary hedge towards a football pitch and a house with a conservatory. Look for a gap in the hedge as you reach the end of the pitch and rejoin the road. Turn right and walk along to Upper Street. As the road bends left, swing right at a footpath sign to Bemerton. Follow the clear path through the trees and eventually you reach a footbridge.

3. Keep right here, cross the Nadder and follow the clear enclosed path between fields, meadows and trees towards Salisbury. Cross a wooden footbridge by a brick cottage and head for several more bridges under some trees. On reaching the entrance to Fitzgerald Farm, turn right and follow the road towards the city centre. There are some striking gabled villas and terraced houses on the left. Cross Cherry Orchard Lane and follow Lower Road. On the right are garages, car showrooms and industrial units. Pass more houses and the railway station before reaching a roundabout.

4. Turn right here and pass the entrance to Fisherton Island; the road soon reaches some detached villas on the left. Keep right at this point and cross the grass, avoiding the footbridge over the Nadder on the right. With the river on your right, make for a footbridge ahead. The bridge crosses a feeder stream. Once across it turn right and take the

Picturesque houses at Salisbury

riverside path along to the confluence of the Nadder and the Avon. Keep left and follow the path along to the next road bridge.

5. Turn right and follow Crane Street to the junction with High Street. Bear right here and walk along to Salisbury Cathedral and the Close. Retrace your steps along Crane Street to the bridge and follow the pretty riverside path by the Avon and the Nadder to the second footbridge. Cross over and follow Town Path across the meadows towards Harnham. Look out along here for cyclists who tend to approach from behind, unseen and unheard. Cross a bridge by Rose Cottage and pass the Old Mill Hotel and Inn. Continue ahead along the road, turn left at Lower Street and return to the car park.

PLACE OF INTEREST NEARBY

In the care of the National Trust, *Mompesson House* by Salisbury Cathedral is a perfect example of Queen Anne architecture. The house contains some notable plasterwork and an elegant carved oak staircase. Fine period furniture is also on display as well as an important collection of 18th century drinking glasses. Telephone: 01722 335659.

For more information about Salisbury and its attractions call the tourist information centre on 01722 334956.

DOWNTON AND THE RIVER AVON

A very enjoyable walk which begins by uncovering Downton's fascinating architectural heritage. From the village the ramble heads north to a private estate and a crumbling family chapel with a fascinating past. Head back to Downton along a delightful stretch of the Avon.

The path across the weir

The sizeable village of Downton has the air of a small town about it and by rights it is a borough. Its long main street runs east-west across the Avon and only a stone's throw away are the woodland glades and sprawling heaths of the New Forest, the largest remaining unspoilt medieval forest in western Europe.

Downton's roots date back to about 1205 when Peter des Roches, Bishop of Winchester, created a new town to the west of the river. When it became a borough, the burgesses paid their rents in cash, instead of holding land against feudal labour and produce. For many years Downton prospered as a centre of industry and commerce. Lace

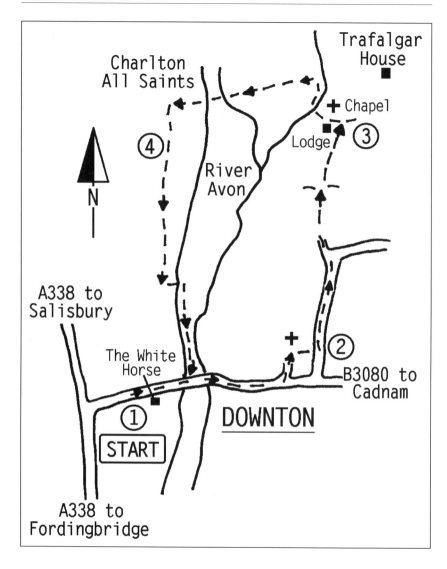

became a cottage industry here and the village has long been associated with flour milling and paper-making. Handmade paper was produced at Downton until the end of the First World War. Along the street, to the east of the Avon, lies the impressive old tannery building, built by the Southern Trading Company in 1919. At the rear of it was a waterwheel, ten feet in diameter. This once-busy industrial site now lies empty.

94

To the north of Downton is Charlton All Saints. There is nothing remarkable about the village itself but a little to the east of it, undisturbed and unseen by passers by on the main road, lies a redundant chapel which is associated with Britain's greatest seafaring hero. Near to the chapel is Trafalgar House, originally called Standlynch House, which dates back to the 18th century and was built by John Wood for Henry Dawkins. The estate was acquired by the Treasury after Dawkins' death in 1814 and given to the heirs of Admiral Viscount Nelson, in gratitude for his services. The house was later occupied by his brother the 1st Earl Nelson and the name of the house changed from Standlynch to Trafalgar. The Nelson family sold the estate to the Duke of Leeds in 1948 when the annuity paid to the Nelson family by the government was terminated. The now abandoned, forlorn place of worship, rebuilt in 1677 and dedicated for use by the Roman Catholic faith in 1914, became the Nelson family's private chapel. Have a look at the crumbling graves and you'll spot the Nelson name.

The walk starts near the 15th century White Horse in Downton, which has recently changed hands. The inn is very spacious inside, with a welcoming atmosphere. It has its own car park at the rear of the building. Telephone for details of the new menu and beers available: 01725 510408.

- **HOW TO GET THERE:** Downton is on the B3080 which runs eastwards off the A338 south of Salisbury.
- **PARKING:** There is room to park in Downton. The area at the front of the White Horse, at the western end of the village, is probably most suitable.
- **LENGTH OF THE WALK:** 4½ miles. Map: OS Landranger 184 Salisbury and The Plain (GR 174214).

THE WALK

1. With your back to the White Horse, turn right and walk through the village of Downton. Cross the River Avon and continue to the turning to the church. Veer left here and approach the lychgate. Keep right and follow the path beside the library to Barford Lane.

2. Turn left and head north out of Downton, passing the cemetery and the Catholic church of the Good Shepherd and Our Blessed Lady Queen of Angels. Cut between pastures and hedgerows and just before the road bends sharp right, veer off to the left and follow a rough rutted track across the fields. Pass over an intersection of tracks and keep ahead. Eventually you reach a lodge set against some trees.

3. Go through a gate and turn left. Pass the Nelson chapel on the right and follow the concrete track as it bends left down to the Avon. Bear right here, by a mill cottage, and take the riverside path across a foaming sluice and weir. Follow the obvious path across the marshes and between reedbeds. Cross several more footbridges and keep ahead over the watermeadows, making for some houses. As you approach them, veer left by clumps of trees in the middle of the field and head for a galvanised gate by a pair of semi-detached houses. Cross two stiles with a track in between and follow the path ahead across the pasture.

4. Follow the path across the fields, crossing several stiles, and make for a concrete track. Go straight on, keeping to the track until it curves towards a large house and some outbuildings. Swing left over a footbridge, then veer right, following the track south towards Downton. The Avon lies over to your left. As you approach the village, the path runs close by the river to pass through a kissing gate. On reaching the road bridge, turn right and return to the car parking area by the White Horse.

PLACE OF INTEREST NEARBY
Breamore House, south of Downton, is a splendid Elizabethan manor house open to the public and containing fine artefacts acquired by ten generations. It was purchased in 1748 by the King's physician, Sir Edward Hulse, and remains in the family today. There was a fire in 1856, ruining the interior but the exterior has remained the same as when it was built in 1583. Telephone: 01725 512468.